EACL Workshop on Semantic Analysis in Social Media 2012

AA005475

Held at the 13th Conference of the European Chapter of the Association for Computational Linguistics (EACL 2012)

Avignon, France
23-24 April 2012

ISBN: 978-1-62276-475-4

Printed from e-media with permission by:

Curran Associates, Inc.
57 Morehouse Lane
Red Hook, NY 12571

CURRAN ASSOCIATES INC.
proceedings.com

Some format issues inherent in the e-media version may also appear in this print version.

Copyright© (2012) by the Association for Computational Linguistics
All rights reserved.

Printed by Curran Associates, Inc. (2013)

For permission requests, please contact the Association for Computational Linguistics at the address below.

Association for Computational Linguistics
209 N. Eighth Street
Stroudsburg, Pennsylvania 18360

Phone: 1-570-476-8006
Fax: 1-570-476-0860

acl@aclweb.org

Additional copies of this publication are available from:

Curran Associates, Inc.
57 Morehouse Lane
Red Hook, NY 12571 USA
Phone: 845-758-0400
Fax: 845-758-2634
Email: curran@proceedings.com
Web: www.proceedings.com

Preface

Semantic analysis in social networks (SN) is important for applications such as understanding and enabling social networks, natural language interfaces and human behaviour on the web, e-learning environments, cyber communities and educational or online shared workspaces. These aspects are also important in security, privacy and identity, opinion mining, sentiment analysis, and in the larger area of affective computing.

This workshop provides a forum for discussion between leading names and researchers involved in text analysis and social networks in the context of natural language understanding, natural language generation, automatic categorization, topic detection, emotion analysis, and applications using computational approaches to process social networks.

Topics of interest include, but are not limited to:

- semantic analysis in sentences and web content from social networks
- classification of texts by emotion and mood from SN
- sociology of emotions and influence on inter-personal communications
- topic detection and clustering in SN
- SN analysis across different languages
- SN analysis from multimedia (text, speech, video)
- security and privacy issues in SNs
- automatic summarization from multiple sources and multiple languages
- analysis of sentiment and opinion in SN
- information extraction and indexing
- applications in which affective aspects are beneficial
- tools and resources for accessing, representing, and managing social network data in natural language processing frameworks (e.g., GATE, UIMA)
- other aspects of the computational treatment of SN and affect.

The workshop covers three main perspectives: government (e.g., security and criminology), industry (e.g., marketing), and academic (e.g., theoretical research related to SNs).

We would like to thank all the authors who submitted papers for the hard work that went behind their submissions. We express our deepest gratitude to the committee members for their thorough reviews. We also thank the EACL 2012 organizers for their help with administrative matters.

Diana Inkpen
Atefeh Farzindar

Organizers:

Atefeh Farzindar (NLP Technologies Inc. and Université de Montréal, Canada)
Diana Inkpen (University of Ottawa, Canada)

Program Committee:

Colin Cherry (National Research Council, Canada)
Viola Ganter (HITS gGmbH, Heidelberg, Germany)
Mitsuru Ishizuka (University of Tokyo, Japan)
Fazel Keshtkar (University of Memphis)
Wael Khreich (NLP Technologies Inc, Canada)
Guy Lapalme (Université de Montréal, Canada)
Eduarda Mendes Rodrigues (University of Porto, Portugal)
Alena Neviarouskaya (Toyohashi University of Technology, Japan)
Alexander Osherenko (Socioware Development, Germany)
Victoria Rubin (University of Western Ontario, Canada)
Carlo Strapparava (FBK-IRST, Povo-Trento, Italy)
Mike Thelwall (University of Wolverhampton, UK)
Alessandro Valitutti (University of Helsinki, Finland)
Simone Teufel (Cambridge University, UK)
René Witte (Concordia University, Canada)

Keynote Speech

Title: Industrial Perspectives on Social Networks

Keynote speaker: Dr. Atefeh Farzindar, NLP Technologies Inc.

Abstract:

Social media data is the collection of open source information that can be obtained publicly via the Web and social networks. Social information intelligence refers to an emerging data and semantic infrastructure that will enable organizations to create a new generation of business applications. This new class of applications will build on the rich set of assets already available within the organization. Social media has become a primary source of intelligence for Security Intelligence and Business Intelligence. Social data intelligence combines social media aspects and analytics to give important business insights, and is a convergence of several trends. Business intelligence from open intelligence incorporates knowledge management, social networking, plus social media monitoring and analytics, all combined into a new interface in the business intelligence environment.

In the context of analyzing social networks, finding powerful methods and algorithms to search for relevant data in large volumes, and various free formats from multiple sources and languages is a scientific challenge. Automatic processing of such data needs to evaluate the appropriate research methods for information extraction, automatic categorization and clustering, indexing data, generating automatic summaries, and statistical machine translation. With respect to machine learning approaches, we must consider developing innovative tools and integrating appropriate linguistic information in the fields of security and defence, and industry business intelligence.

There is great interest for social media data monitoring in the industry. Social media data can dramatically improve business intelligence and help both international and local markets. Businesses could achieve several goals by integrating social data into their corporate BI systems, such as branding and awareness, customer/prospect engagement and improving customer service.

Biography:

Dr. Atefeh Farzindar is the founder of NLP Technologies Inc., a company specializing in natural language processing, automatic summarization, statistical machine translation and social media solutions. Dr. Farzindar received her Ph.D. in Computer Science from the Université de Montréal and Paris-Sorbonne University. She is an adjunct professor at the Department of Computer Science at the Université de Montréal. As president of NLP Technologies, she has managed multiple collaborative R&D projects with various industry and university partners. She is the chair of the language technologies sector of the Language Industry Association Canada (AILIA) and a board member of the Language Technologies Research Centre, co-chair of the Canadian Conference on Artificial Intelligence 2010 and industry chair for Canadian AI'2011 and AI'2012.

Invited Talk

Title: Mining Online Discussions: An Applications to the Analysis of News Websites

Invited Speaker: Dr. Julien Velcin, Associate Professor in CS, ERIC Lab - University of Lyon

Abstract:

News stories websites represent an important source of data for building a picture of what is going on in the world. Apart from providing the information itself, such websites allow Internet users to post their opinions and comments in the form of discussions.

These discussions bring valuable knowledge in order to understand a person's position regarding certain news. In the first part of the talk, I will briefly present this type of data and explain how they represent a challenge. After this introduction, I will discuss the content-oriented model as well as the recommended system we have developed for analyzing key messages posted in such online discussions. In addition, I will present the approach we have followed for extracting the implicit users' network. To this end, I will focus on a model involving three types of relations, two of which are based on the citations. The resulting user network is seen as an implicit social network and I will explain how it can be used to extract celebrities. Finally, I will introduce the problem of image extraction addressed in a new project, where an image is seen as a representation of various entities populating the Internet (e.g., politicians, companies, brands etc.). In particular, I will show how this kind of project interrelates traditional text/opinion mining with social network analysis.

Biography:

After his MSc graduation in Artificial Intelligence and Pattern Recognition (2002), Julien Velcin defended a PhD in Computer Science at the University of Paris 6 in 2005. He is a researcher in the ERIC Lab, University of Lyon 2 since 2007. His research interests lie mainly in the extraction, evaluation and characterization of categories in unsupervised machine learning, with applications to text mining and web analysis. His work has been published in international journals and conferences such as WIAS, IJCAI, ICCS, ISMIS, ER. He is involved in international program committees such as ECML-PKDD, ASONAM, and EGC. He is a member of the editorial board of the International Journal of Data Analysis Techniques and Strategies (IJDATS). He is an active reviewer for the Association for Computing Machinery (ACM) since 2009. He is currently project manager of a national project on the study of images and opinion evolution through the Internet, funded by the French National Research Agency.

Table of Contents

Unsupervised Part-of-Speech Tagging in Noisy and Esoteric Domains With a Syntactic-Semantic Bayesian HMM
William M. Darling, Michael J. Paul and Fei Song 1

The Role of Emotional Stability in Twitter Conversations
Fabio Celli and Luca Rossi 10

Towards Scalable Speech Act Recognition in Twitter: Tackling Insufficient Training Data
Renxian Zhang, Dehong Gao and Wenjie Li 18

Topic Classification of Blog Posts Using Distant Supervision
Stephanie Husby and Denilson Barbosa 28

A User and NLP-Assisted Strategic Workflow for a Social Semantic OWL 2-Based Knowledge Platform
Jinan El-Hachem and Volker Haarslev 37

A Hybrid Framework for Scalable Opinion Mining in Social Media: Detecting Polarities and Attitude Targets
Carlos Rodriguez-Penagos, Jens Grivolla and Joan Codina-Filba 46

Predicting the 2011 Dutch Senate Election Results with Twitter
Erik Tjong Kim Sang and Johan Bos 53

Opinion and Suggestion Analysis for Expert Recommendations
Anna Stavrianou and Caroline Brun 61

Conference Program

Monday, April 23, 2012

9:00–9:10	Opening Remarks by Diana Inkpen, University of Ottawa
9:10–9:30	Keynote speech: Industrial Perspectives on Social Networks by Atefeh Farzindar, NLP Technologies
9:30–10:00	*Unsupervised Part-of-Speech Tagging in Noisy and Esoteric Domains With a Syntactic-Semantic Bayesian HMM* William M. Darling, Michael J. Paul and Fei Song
10:00–10:30	Coffee break
10:30–11:00	*The Role of Emotional Stability in Twitter Conversations* Fabio Celli and Luca Rossi
11:00–11:30	*Towards Scalable Speech Act Recognition in Twitter: Tackling Insufficient Training Data* Renxian Zhang, Dehong Gao and Wenjie Li
11:30–12:00	*Topic Classification of Blog Posts Using Distant Supervision* Stephanie Husby and Denilson Barbosa
12:00–12:30	*A User and NLP-Assisted Strategic Workflow for a Social Semantic OWL 2-Based Knowledge Platform* Jinan El-Hachem and Volker Haarslev
12:30-14:00	Lunch break
14:00-15:00	Invited talk: Mining Online Discussions: an Application to the Analysis of News Websites by Julien Velcin, University Lyon 2
15:00-15:30	*A Hybrid Framework for Scalable Opinion Mining in Social Media: Detecting Polarities and Attitude Targets* Carlos Rodriguez-Penagos, Jens Grivolla and Joan Codina-Filba
15:30-16:00	Coffee break
16:00-16:30	*Predicting the 2011 Dutch Senate Election Results with Twitter* Erik Tjong Kim Sang and Johan Bos
16:30-17:00	*Opinion and Suggestion Analysis for Expert Recommendations* Anna Stavrianou and Caroline Brun

Monday, April 23, 2012 (continued)

17:00-17:30 Closing Remarks and Discussion

Unsupervised Part-of-Speech Tagging in Noisy and Esoteric Domains with a Syntactic-Semantic Bayesian HMM

William M. Darling
School of Computer Science
University of Guelph
wdarling@uoguelph.ca

Michael J. Paul
Dept. of Computer Science
Johns Hopkins University
mpaul@cs.jhu.edu

Fei Song
School of Computer Science
University of Guelph
fsong@uoguelph.ca

Abstract

Unsupervised part-of-speech (POS) tagging has recently been shown to greatly benefit from Bayesian approaches where HMM parameters are integrated out, leading to significant increases in tagging accuracy. These improvements in unsupervised methods are important especially in specialized social media domains such as Twitter where little training data is available. Here, we take the Bayesian approach one step further by integrating semantic information from an LDA-like topic model with an HMM. Specifically, we present *Part-of-Speech LDA* (POSLDA), a syntactically and semantically consistent generative probabilistic model. This model discovers POS specific topics from an unlabelled corpus. We show that this model consistently achieves improvements in unsupervised POS tagging and language modeling over the Bayesian HMM approach with varying amounts of side information in the noisy and esoteric domain of Twitter.

1 Introduction

The explosion of social media in recent years has led to the need for NLP tools like part-of-speech (POS) taggers that are robust enough to handle data that is becoming increasingly "noisy." Unfortunately, many NLP systems fail at out-of-domain data and struggle with the informal style of social text. With spelling errors, abbreviations, uncommon acronyms, and excessive use of slang, systems that are designed for traditional corpora such as news articles may perform poorly when given difficult input such as a Twitter feed (Ritter et al., 2010).

Recognizing the limitations of existing systems, Gimpel et al. (2011) develop a POS tagger specifically for Twitter, by creating a training corpus as well as devising a tag set that includes parts of speech that are uniquely found in online language, such as emoticons (smilies). This is an important step forward, but a POS tagger tailored to Twitter cannot tackle the social Web as a whole. Other online communities have their own styles, slang, memes, and other idiosyncrasies, so a system trained for one community may not apply to others.

For example, the 140-character limit of Twitter encourages abbreviations and word-dropping that may not be found in less restrictive venues. The first-person subject is often assumed in "status messages" that one finds in Twitter and Facebook, so the pronominal subject can be dropped, even in English (Weir, 2012), leading to messages like "Went out" instead of "I went out." Not only does Twitter follow these unusual grammatical patterns, but many messages contain "hashtags" which could be considered their own syntactic class not found in other data sources. For these reasons, POS parameters learned from Twitter data will not necessarily fit other social data.

In general, concerns about the limitations of domain-dependent models have motivated the use of sophisticated unsupervised methods. Interest in unsupervised POS induction has been revived in recent years after Bayesian HMMs are shown to increase accuracy by up to 14 percentage points over basic maximum-likelihood estimation (Goldwater and Griffiths, 2007). Despite falling well short of the accuracy obtained with supervised taggers, unsupervised approaches are preferred in situations where there is no access to

Proceedings of the 13th Conference of the European Chapter of the Association for Computational Linguistics, pages 1–9,
Avignon, France, April 23 - 27 2012. ©2012 Association for Computational Linguistics

large quantities of training data in a specific domain, which is increasingly common with Web data. We therefore hope to continue improving accuracy with unsupervised approaches by introducing semantics as an additional source of information for this task.

The ambiguities of language are amplified through social media, where new words or spellings of words are routinely invented. For example, "ow" on Twitter can be a shorthand for "how," in addition to its more traditional use as an expression of pain (ouch). While POS assignment is inherently a problem of **syntactic** disambiguation, we hypothesize that the underlying **semantic** content can aid the disambiguation task. If we know that the overall content of a message is about police, then the word "cop" is likely to be a noun, whereas if the context is about shopping, this could be slang for acquiring or stealing (verb). The HMM approach will often be able to tag these occurrences appropriately given the context, but in many cases the syntactic context may be limited or misleading due to the noisy nature of the data. Thus, we believe that semantic context will offer additional evidence toward making an accurate prediction.

Following this intuition, this paper presents a semantically and syntactically coherent Bayesian model that uncovers POS-specific sub-topics within general semantic topics, as in latent Dirichlet allocation (LDA) (Blei et al., 2003), which we call **part-of-speech LDA**, or POSLDA. The resulting posterior distributions will reflect specialized topics such as "verbs about dining" or "nouns about politics". To the best of our knowledge, we also present the first experiments with unsupervised tagging for a social media corpus. In this work, we focus on Twitter because the labeled corpus by Gimpel et al. (2011) allows us to quantitatively evaluate our approach. We demonstrate the model's utility as a predictive language model by its low perplexity on held-out test data as compared to several related topic models, and most importantly, we show that this model achieves statistically significant and consistent improvements in unsupervised POS tagging accuracy over a Bayesian HMM. These results support our hypothesis that semantic information can directly improve the quality of POS induction, and our experiments present an in-depth exploration of this task on informal social text.

The next section discusses related work, which is followed by a description of our model, POSLDA. We then present POS tagging results on the Twitter POS dataset (Gimpel et al., 2011). Section 5 describes further experiments on the POSLDA model and section 6 includes a discussion on the results and why POSLDA can do better on POS tagging than a vanilla Bayesian HMM. Finally, section 7 concludes with a discussion on future work.

2 Related Work

Modern unsupervised POS tagging originates with Merialdo (1993) who trained a trigram HMM using maximum likelihood estimation (MLE). Goldwater and Griffiths (2007) improved upon this approach by treating the HMM in a Bayesian sense; the rows of the transition matrix are random variables with proper Bayesian priors and the state emission probabilities are also random variables with their own priors. The posterior distribution of tags is learned using Gibbs sampling and this model improves in accuracy over the MLE approach by up to 14 percentage points.

In the "Topics and Syntax" model (or HMMLDA), the generative process of a corpus is cast as a composite model where syntax is modeled with an HMM and semantics are modeled with LDA (Griffiths et al., 2005). Here, one state of an HMM is replaced with a topic model such that the words with long-range dependencies ("content" words) will be drawn from a set of topics. The remaining states are reserved for "syntax" words that exhibit only short-range dependencies. Griffiths et al. (2005) briefly touch on POS tagging with their model, but its superiority to a plain Bayesian HMM is not shown and the authors note that this is partially because all semantic-like words get assigned to the single semantic class in their model. This misses the distinction between at least nouns and verbs, but many other semantic-dependent words as well. If more variation could be provided in the semantic portion of the model, the POS tagging results would likely improve.

3 Part-of-Speech LDA (POSLDA)

In their canonical form, topic models do not capture local dependencies between words (i.e. syntactic relations), but they do capture long-range

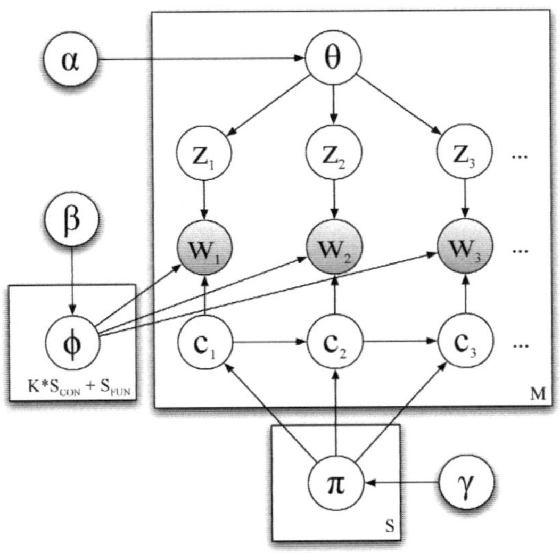

Figure 1: Graphical model depiction of POSLDA.

context such as the overall topical content or gist of a document. Conversely, under an HMM, words are assumed completely independent of their broader context by the Markov assumption. We seek to bridge these restrictions with our unified model, Part-of-Speech LDA (POSLDA).

Under this model, each word token is now associated with two latent variables: a semantic topic z and a syntactic class c. We posit that the topics are generated through the LDA process, while the classes are generated through an HMM. The observed word tokens are then dependent on both the topic and the class: rather than a single multinomial for a particular topic z or a particular class c, there are distributions for each topic-class pair (z, c) from which we assume words are sampled.

We denote the set of classes $\mathcal{C} = \mathcal{C}_{\text{CON}} \cup \mathcal{C}_{\text{FUN}}$, which includes the set of content or "semantic" classes $\mathcal{C}_{\text{CON}}$ for word types such as nouns and verbs that depend on the current topic, and functional or "syntactic-only" classes $\mathcal{C}_{\text{FUN}}$. If a word is generated from a functional class, it does not depend on the topic. This allows our model to accommodate functional words like determiners which appear independently of the topical content of a document.

We use the same notation as LDA, where θ is a document-topic distribution and ϕ is a topic-word distribution. Additionally, we denote the HMM transition rows as π, which we assume is drawn from a Dirichlet with hyperparameter γ. Denote $S = |\mathcal{C}|$ and $K = |\mathcal{Z}|$, the numbers of classes and topics, respectively. There are S_{FUN} word distributions $\phi^{(\text{FUN})}$ for function word classes and $K \times S_{\text{CON}}$ word distributions $\phi^{(\text{CON})}$ for content word classes. A graphical model depiction of POSLDA is shown in Figure 1.

Thus, the generative process of a corpus can be described as:

1. Draw $\pi \sim \text{Dirichlet}(\gamma)$
2. Draw $\phi \sim \text{Dirichlet}(\beta)$
3. For each document $d \in \mathcal{D}$:
   (a) Draw $\theta_d \sim \text{Dirichlet}(\alpha)$
   (b) For each word token $w_i \in d$:
      i. Draw $c_i \sim \pi_{c_{i-1}}$
      ii. If $c_i \notin \mathcal{C}_{\text{CON}}$:
         A. Draw $w_i \sim \phi^{(\text{FUN})}_{c_i}$
      iii. Else:
         A. Draw $z_i \sim \theta_d$
         B. Draw $w_i \sim \phi^{(\text{CON})}_{c_i,z_i}$

In topic models, it is generally true that common function words may overwhelm the word distributions, leading to suboptimal results that are difficult to interpret. This is usually accommodated by data pre-processing (e.g. stop word removal), by backing off to "background" word models (Chemudugunta et al., 2006), or by performing term re-weighting (Wilson and Chew, 2010). In the case of POSLDA, these common words are naturally captured by the functional classes.

3.1 Relations to Other Models

The idea of having multinomials for the cross products of topics and classes is related to multifaceted topic models where word tokens are associated with multiple latent variables (Paul and Girju, 2010; Ahmed and Xing, 2010). Under such models, words can be explained by a latent topic as well as a second underlying variable such as the perspective or dialect of the author, and words may depend on both factors. In our case, the second variable is the part-of-speech – or functional purpose – of the token.

We note that POSLDA is a generalization of many existing models. POSLDA becomes a Bayesian HMM when the number of topics $K = 1$; the original LDA model when the number of classes $S = 1$; and the HMMLDA model of Griffiths et al. (2005) when the number of content word classes $S_{\text{CON}} = 1$. The beauty of these generalizations is that one can easily experiment with any of these models by simply altering the model parameters under a single POSLDA implementation.

3.2 Inference

As with many complex probabilistic models, exact posterior inference is intractable for POSLDA. Nevertheless, a number of approximate inference techniques are at our disposal. In this work, we use collapsed Gibbs sampling to sample the latent class assignments and topic assignments ($\mathbf{c}$ and $\mathbf{z}$), and from these we can compute estimates of the multinomial parameters for the topics (ϕ), the document-topic portions (θ), and the HMM transition matrix (π). Under a trigram version of the model – which we employ for all our experiments in this work – the sampling equation for word token i is as follows:

$$p(c_i, z_i | \mathbf{c_{-i}}, \mathbf{z_{-i}}, \mathbf{w}) \propto$$

$$\begin{cases} \rho_{c_i} \times \frac{n^{(d)}_{z_i} + \alpha_{z_i}}{n^{(d)}_{\cdot} + \alpha_{\cdot}} \frac{n^{(c_i, z_i)}_{w} + \beta}{n^{(c_i, z_i)}_{\cdot} + W\beta} & c_i \in S_{\text{CON}} \\ \rho_{c_i} \times \frac{n^{(c_i)}_{w} + \beta}{n^{(c_i)}_{\cdot} + W\beta} & c_i \in S_{\text{FUN}} \end{cases}$$

where

$$\rho_{c_i} = \frac{n_{(c_{i-2}, c_{i-1}, c_i)} + \gamma_{c_i}}{n_{(c_{i-2}, c_{i-1})} + \gamma_{\cdot}} \cdot \frac{n_{(c_{i-1}, c_i, c_{i+1})} + \gamma_{c_i}}{n_{(c_{i-1}, c_i)} + \gamma_{\cdot}} \cdot \frac{n_{(c_i, c_{i+1}, c_{i+2})} + \gamma_{c_i}}{n_{(c_i, c_{i+1})} + \gamma_{\cdot}}$$

Although we sample the pair (c_i, z_i) jointly as a block, which requires computing a sampling distribution over $S_{\text{FUN}} + K \times S_{\text{CON}}$, it is also valid to sample c_i and z_i separately, which requires only $S + K$ computations. In this case, the sampling procedure would be somewhat different. Despite the lower number of computations per iteration, however, the sampler is likely to converge faster with our blocked approach because the two variables are tightly coupled. The intuition is that a non-block-based sampler could have difficulty escaping local optima because we are interested in the most probable *pair*; a highly probable class c sampled on its own, for example, could prevent the sampler from choosing a more likely pair (c', z).

4 POS Tagging Experiments

To demonstrate the veracity of our approach, we performed a number of POS tagging experiments using the POSLDA model. Our data is the recent Twitter POS dataset released at ACL 2011 by Gimpel et al. (2011) consisting of approximately 26,000 words across 1,827 tweets. This dataset provides a unique opportunity to test our unsupervised approach in a domain where it would likely be of most use – one that is novel and therefore lacking large amounts of training data. We feel that this sort of specialized domain will become the norm – particularly in social media analysis – as user generated content continues to grow in size and accessibility. The Twitter dataset uses a domain-dependent tag set of 25 tags that are described in (Gimpel et al., 2011).

For our experiments, we follow the established form of Merialdo (1993) and Goldwater and Griffiths (2007) for unsupervised POS tagging by making use of a tag dictionary to constrain the possible tag choices for each word and therefore render the problem closer to disambiguation. Like Goldwater and Griffiths (2007), we employ a number of dictionaries with varying degrees of knowledge.

We use the full corpus of tweets[1] and construct a tag dictionary which contains the tag information for a word only when it appears more than d times in the corpus. We ran experiments for $d = 1, 2, 3, 5, 10$, and ∞ where the problem becomes POS clustering. We report both tagging accuracy and the variation of information (VI), which computes the information lost in moving from one clustering C to another C': $VI(C, C') = H(C) + H(C') - 2I(C, C')$ (Meilă, 2007). This can be interpreted as a measure of similarity between the clusterings, where a smaller value indicates higher similarity.

We run our Gibbs sampler for 20,000 iterations and obtain a maximum a posteriori (MAP) estimate for each word's tag by employing simulated annealing. Each posterior probability $p(c, z|\cdot)$ in the sampling distribution is raised to the power of $\frac{1}{\tau}$ where τ is a temperature that approaches 0 as the sampler converges. This approach is akin to

[1]The Twitter POS dataset consists of three subsets of tweets: development, training, and testing. Because we are performing fully unsupervised tagging, however, we combine these three subsets into one.

Accuracy	1	2	3	5	10	∞
random	62.8	49.6	45.2	40.2	35.0	
BHMM	78.4	65.4	59.0	51.8	44.0	
POSLDA	**80.9**	**67.5**	**62.0**	**55.9**	**47.6**	
VI						
random	2.34	3.31	3.56	3.81	4.05	5.86
BHMM	1.41	2.47	2.84	3.22	3.61	5.07
POSLDA	**1.30**	**2.34**	**2.66**	**2.98**	**3.35**	**4.96**
Corpus stats						
% ambig.	54.2	67.9	72.2	76.4	80.4	100
tags / token	2.62	5.91	7.19	8.59	10.3	25

Table 1: POS tagging results on Twitter dataset.

K	Accuracy	σ
1 (HMM)	78.6	0.23
5	80.0	0.06
10	80.9	0.17
15	80.1	0.10
20	80.2	0.21
25	80.1	0.25
30	80.2	0.15
35	80.1	0.12
40	79.9	0.20
45	80.1	0.12

Table 2: POS tagging results as K varies on Twitter dataset.

bringing a system from an arbitrary state to one with the lowest energy, thus viewing the Gibbs sampling procedure as a random search whose goal is to identify the MAP tag sequence – a technique that is also employed by Goldwater and Griffiths (2007). Finally, we run each experiment 5 times from random initializations and report the average accuracy and variation of information.

4.1 Results for Twitter Dataset

In our experiments, we use 8 content classes that correspond to the following parts-of-speech: noun, proper noun, proper noun + possessive, proper noun + verbal, verb, adjective, adverb, and other abbreviations / foreign words. We chose these classes because intuitively they are the types of words whose generative probability will depend on the given latent topic. As the Twitter POS data consists of 25 distinct tags, this leaves 17 remaining classes for function words. In this section, we report results for $K = 10$ topics. We will discuss the effect of varying K in section 4.2. We set symmetric priors with $\alpha = 1.0/K = 0.1$, $\beta = 0.5$, and $\gamma = 0.01$.

As is demonstrated in Table 1, our POSLDA model shows marked improvements over a random tag assignment and, more importantly, the Bayesian HMM approach described by Goldwater and Griffiths (2007). It does so for every setting of d on both accuracy and variation of information. For $d = 1$ our method outperforms the BHMM by 2.5 percentage points. With higher values of d, however, POSLDA increases its improvement over the BHMM to up to 4.1 percentage points. The increase in tagging accuracy as d increases suggests that our method may be particularly suitable for domains with little training data.[2] For $d = \infty$, where we are performing POS *clustering*, our model improves the variation of information by 0.11. Each of these improvements over the Bayesian HMM is statistically significant with $p \ll 0.01$. Despite the clear improvements in POS tagging accuracy and clustering that we demonstrate in this section, we trained our POSLDA model with a "blind" topic setting of $K = 10$. In the following section, we will investigate how this parameter affects the achievable results with our technique.

4.2 Topic Variance

In the previous section we set the number of topics *a priori* to $K = 10$. However, it is well known in topic modeling research that different datasets exhibit different numbers of "inherent" topics (Blei et al., 2003). Therefore, a POSLDA model fit with the "correct" number of topics will likely achieve higher accuracy in POS tagging. A standard approach to tuning the number of topics to fit a topic model is to try a number of different topics and choose the one that results in the lowest perplexity on a held-out test set (Claeskens and Hjort, 2008). Here, we can choose the optimal K more directly by trying a number of different values and choosing the one that maximizes the POS tagging accuracy.

For this experiment, we again make use of the Twitter POS dataset (Gimpel et al., 2011). We use the same setup as that described above with simulated annealing, 20,000 iterations, and a tag dic-

[2] The differences in tagging accuracy in terms of percentage points between POSLDA and the BHMM for $d = \{1, 2, 3, 5, 10\}$ are $\Delta_a = \{2.5, 2.1, 3.0, 4.1, 3.6\}$, respectively. For clustering, the increases in VI are even more clear as d increases. They are $\Delta_{VI} = \{0.11, 0.13, 0.18, 0.24, 0.26\}$.

tionary with $d = 1$. As before, we set $\alpha = 1.0/K$, $\beta = 0.5$, and $\gamma = 0.01$. We perform experiments with $K = \{1, 5, 10, \ldots, 40, 45\}$, where $K = 1$ corresponds to the Bayesian HMM. The results averaged over 3 runs are tabulated in Table 2 with the associated standard deviations (σ), and shown graphically in Figure 2.

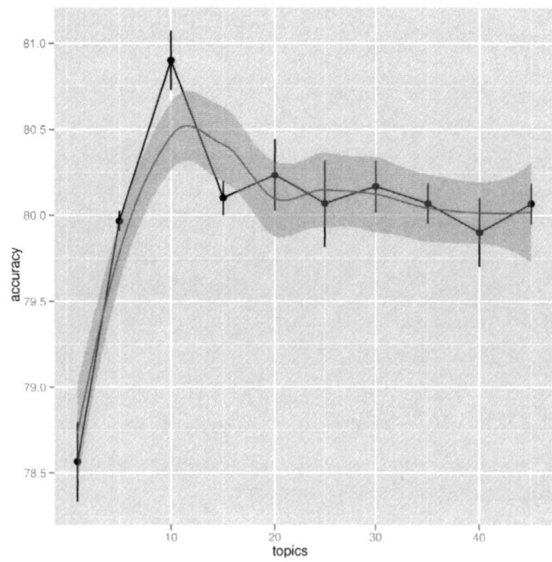

Figure 2: Number of topics K vs. POS tagging accuracy on the Twitter dataset. The average accuracies, along with their standard errors, are shown in black, while a smoothed curve of the same data is shown in blue.

As we expect, the tagging accuracy depends on the number of topics specified by the model. In fact, the accuracy improves by nearly a full percentage point from both the previous and next topic settings when we hit a critical point at $K = 10$. When $K = 1$ the model reduces to the Bayesian HMM and our accuracy suffers. It steadily increases until we hit the critical point and then drops off again but plateaus at a level that is approximately 1.5 percentage points higher than the BHMM. This shows that determining an appropriate setting for the number of topics is essential for the best possible tagging accuracy using POSLDA. Nevertheless, even with a "blind" setting within a large range of topic values (here from $K = 5$ to at least $K = 45$), we see marked improvements over the baseline system that does not include any semantic topic information.

5 Model Evaluation

In this section we present further experiments on the raw output of POSLDA to demonstrate its capabilities beyond simply POS tagging. We show the model's ability both qualitatively and quantitatively to capture the semantic (or "content") and syntactic (or "functional") axes of information prevalent in a corpus made up of social media data. We begin qualitatively with topic interpretability when the model is learned given a collection of unannotated Twitter messages, and then present quantitative results on the ability of POSLDA as a predictive language model in the Twitter domain.

5.1 Topic Interpretability

Judging the interpretability of a set of topics is highly subjective, and there are understandably various differing approaches of evaluating topic cohesiveness. For example, Chang et al. (2009) look at "word intrusion" where a user determines an *intruding* word from a set of words that does not thematically fit with the other words, and "topic intrusion" where a user determines whether the learned document-topic portion θ_d appropriately describes the semantic theme of the document. In this section, we are most interested in subjectively demonstrating the low incidence of "word intrusion" both in terms of semantics (theme) and syntax (part-of-speech). We do not conduct formal experiments to demonstrate this, but we subjectively show that our model learns semantic and syntactic word distributions that are likely robust towards problems of word intrusion and that are therefore "interpretable" for humans examining the learned posterior word distributions.

Table 3 shows three topics – manually labelled as "party", "status update", and "politics" – learned from the relatively small Twitter POS dataset. We set the number of topics $K = 20$, the number of classes $S = 25$, and the number of content word classes $S_{\text{CON}} = 8$, following our earlier POS tagging experiments. We show the top five words from three POS-specific topics labelled manually as *noun*, *verb*, and *adjective*. Given the relatively small size of the dataset, the short length of the documents, and the esoteric language and grammar use, the interpretability of the topics is reasonable. All three topics assign high probability to words that one would

PARTY			STATUS UPDATE			POLITICS		
noun	*verb*	*adj*	*noun*	*verb*	*adj*	*noun*	*verb*	*adj*
party	gets	awesome	day	is	nice	anything	say	late
man	is	old	pm	looking	nasty	truth	has	real
shit	knew	original	school	so	last	face	wait	high
men	were	fake	today	have	hard	city	cant	republican
person	wasnt	drunk	body	got	tired	candidate	going	important

Table 3: Example topics learned from the Twitter POS dataset with POSLDA.

CONJ	DET	PREP	RP
and	the	to	to
but	a	of	it
or	my	in	up
n	your	for	away
in	this	on	in
yet	that	with	on
plus	is	at	around
nd	some	NUMBER	out
an	an	if	over
to	his	from	off

Table 4: Example topic-independent function class distributions ($\mathcal{C}_{\text{FUN}}$) learned from the Twitter POS dataset with POSLDA.

expect to have high importance with one or two outliers. More importantly, however, the POS-specific topics also generally reflect their syntactic roles. Each of the verbs is assuredly (even without the proper context) a verb (with the single outlier being the word "so"), and the same thing for the nouns. The adjectives seem to fit as well; though many of the words could be considered nouns depending on the context, it is clear how given the topic each of the words could very well act as an adjective. A final point worth mentioning is that, unlike LDA, we do not perform stopword removal. Instead, the POSLDA model has pushed stopwords to their own *function* classes (rather than content) freeing us from having to perform pre- or post-processing steps to ensure interpretable topics. The top words in four of these topic-independent function classes, learned from the Twitter POS dataset, are shown in Table 4.[3] These function word distributions are even more cohesive than the content word distributions, showing that the standard stopwords have been accounted for as we expect in their respective function classes.

[3]Note that we make use of the tag dictionary when learning these word distributions.

5.2 Predictive Language Modeling

While we have demonstrated that our model can achieve improved accuracy in POS tagging for Twitter data, it can also be useful for other kinds of language analysis in the social media domain. In the following experiments, we test the POSLDA model quantitatively by determining its ability as a predictive language model. Following a standard practice in topic modeling research (Blei et al., 2003; Griffiths et al., 2005), we fit a model to a training set and then compute the perplexity of a held-out test set. For this experiment, we use the Twitter POS *training* dataset described earlier (16,348 words across 999 tweets). We then perform testing on the Twitter POS *testing* dataset (8,027 words across 500 tweets). We compare the perplexity – a monotonically decreasing function of the log likelihood – to LDA, a Bayesian HMM, and HMMLDA. Finally, we use Minka's fixed-point method (Wallach, 2008) to optimize the hyperparameters α and β.

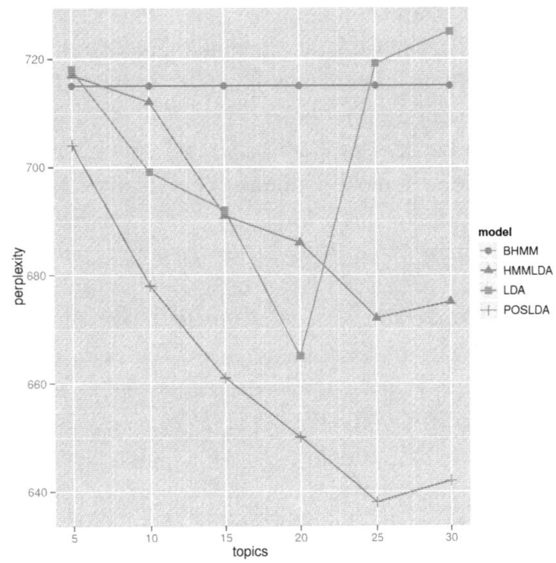

Figure 3: Perplexity of POSLDA and other probabilistic models.

Figure 3 shows the perplexity on the held-out Twitter test set for models trained with $K = \{5, 10, 15, 20, 25, 30\}$. The Bayesian HMM is not affected by the number of topics and is able to beat the HMMLDA model at $K = 5$. It also achieves lower perplexity than the LDA model at $K = 5, 25$, and 30. Our POSLDA model, however, achieves the lowest perplexity of all tested models at all topic settings that we tested. This demonstrates that POSLDA is a good candidate for both language modeling and for further latent probabilistic model-based analysis of Twitter data.

6 Discussion

In the previous section we demonstrated both qualitatively and quantitatively that our model captures two sources of information from unstructured texts: thematic (or semantics) and functional (or syntactic). An important question to consider is why – as we demonstrated in section 4 – learning this sort of information improves our ability to perform unsupervised POS tagging. One reason is discussed in the introduction: semantic information can help disambiguate the POS for a word that typically serves a different function depending on the topic that it is normally associated with. This phenomenon likely plays an important role in the accuracy improvements that we observe. However, another feature of the model is the distinction between "content" POS classes and "function" POS classes. The former will depend on the current topic while the latter are universal across thematic space. This will also represent an improvement over the bare HMM because words that depend on the current topic – typically nouns, verbs, adjectives, and adverbs – will be forced to these classes due to their long-range thematic dependencies while words with only short-range dependencies will be pushed to the function POS classes. This latter type of words – conjunctions, determiners, etc. – naturally do not depend on themes so as they are pushed to the function-only POS classes, and so one step of disambiguation has already been performed. This is the same behaviour as in the HMMLDA model by Griffiths et al. (2005), but here we are able to perform proper POS tagging because there is more than just a single content word class and we are therefore able to discern between the topic-dependent parts-of-speech.

7 Conclusions and Future Work

In this paper, we have shown that incorporating semantic topic information into a Bayesian HMM can result in impressive increases in accuracy for unsupervised POS tagging. Specifically, we presented POSLDA – a topic model consistent across the axes of both semantic and syntactic meanings. Using this model to perform unsupervised POS tagging results in consistent and statistically significant increases in POS tagging accuracy and decreases in variation of information when performing POS clustering. These improvements are demonstrated on a novel release of data from the microblogging social network site Twitter. This type of dataset is of particular interest because unsupervised POS tagging will likely be most important in specialized idiosyncratic domains with atypical features and small amounts of labelled training data. Crucially, we showed that even with the inconsistent and at times strange use of grammar, slang, and acronyms, the syntactic portion of the model demonstrably improves not only the predictive ability of the model in terms of perplexity, but also the accuracy in unsupervised POS tagging. This is important because in general tweets are far from being representative of "proper" grammar. Nevertheless, there clearly exists some adherence to syntactic structure as the use of the HMM within our model improves word prediction and POS tagging.

This work represents the first – to our knowledge – application of latent thematic information to the unsupervised POS tagging task.[4] However, due to the encouraging results, there are a number of future research directions that present themselves from this work. One immediate task is to extend POSLDA to a nonparametric Bayesian model. Section 4.2 shows how varying the number of topics K in the model can affect the tagging accuracy by up to a full percentage point. A nonparametric version of the model would free us from having to perform the initial model selection step to get the best accuracy. Another avenue for future work is to infuse more structure into the model such as word morphology.

[4]There has been some work done to include semantic information collected separately in a *supervised* POS tagging approach (Toutanova and Johnson, 2008).

Acknowledgments

William Darling is supported by an NSERC Doctoral Postgraduate Scholarship, and Michael Paul is supported by an NSF Graduate Research Fellowship. The authors would like to thank the anonymous reviewers for their helpful comments and suggestions.

References

Amr Ahmed and Eric P. Xing. 2010. Staying informed: supervised and semi-supervised multi-view topical analysis of ideological perspective. In *Proceedings of the 2010 Conference on Empirical Methods in Natural Language Processing*, EMNLP '10, pages 1140–1150, Stroudsburg, PA, USA. Association for Computational Linguistics.

David M. Blei, Andrew Y. Ng, and Michael I. Jordan. 2003. Latent dirichlet allocation. *J. Mach. Learn. Res.*, 3:993–1022.

Jonathan Chang, Jordan Boyd-Graber, Chong Wang, Sean Gerrish, and David M. Blei. 2009. Reading tea leaves: How humans interpret topic models. In *Neural Information Processing Systems*.

Chaitanya Chemudugunta, Padhraic Smyth, and Mark Steyvers. 2006. Modeling general and specific aspects of documents with a probabilistic topic model. In *NIPS*, pages 241–248.

G. Claeskens and N.L. Hjort. 2008. *Model Selection and Model Averaging*. Cambridge University Press.

Kevin Gimpel, Nathan Schneider, Brendan O'Connor, Dipanjan Das, Daniel Mills, Jacob Eisenstein, Michael Heilman, Dani Yogatama, Jeffrey Flanigan, and Noah A. Smith. 2011. Part-of-speech tagging for twitter: Annotation, features, and experiments. In *Proceedings of the Annual Meeting of the Association for Computational Linguistics*.

Sharon Goldwater and Tom Griffiths. 2007. A fully Bayesian approach to unsupervised part-of-speech tagging. In *Proceedings of the 45th Annual Meeting of the Association of Computational Linguistics*, pages 744–751. Association for Computational Linguistics.

Thomas L. Griffiths, Mark Steyvers, David M. Blei, and Joshua B. Tenenbaum. 2005. Integrating topics and syntax. In *In Advances in Neural Information Processing Systems 17*, pages 537–544. MIT Press.

Donna Harman. 1992. Overview of the first text retrieval conference (trec-1). In *TREC*, pages 1–20.

M. Meilă. 2007. Comparing clusteringsan information based distance. *Journal of Multivariate Analysis*, 98(5):873–895, May.

Bernard Merialdo. 1993. Tagging english text with a probabilistic model. *Computational Linguistics*, 20:155–171.

Michael J. Paul and Roxana Girju. 2010. A two-dimensional topic-aspect model for discovering multi-faceted topics. In *AAAI*.

Alan Ritter, Colin Cherry, and Bill Dolan. 2010. Unsupervised modeling of twitter conversations. In *Human Language Technologies: The 2010 Annual Conference of the North American Chapter of the Association for Computational Linguistics*, HLT '10, pages 172–180, Stroudsburg, PA, USA. Association for Computational Linguistics.

Noah A. Smith and Jason Eisner. 2005. Contrastive estimation: training log-linear models on unlabeled data. In *Proceedings of the 43rd Annual Meeting on Association for Computational Linguistics*, ACL '05, pages 354–362, Stroudsburg, PA, USA. Association for Computational Linguistics.

Kristina Toutanova and Mark Johnson. 2008. A bayesian lda-based model for semi-supervised part-of-speech tagging. In J.C. Platt, D. Koller, Y. Singer, and S. Roweis, editors, *Advances in Neural Information Processing Systems 20*, pages 1521–1528. MIT Press, Cambridge, MA.

Hanna Wallach, David Mimno, and Andrew McCallum. 2009. Rethinking lda: Why priors matter. In *NIPS*.

Hanna M. Wallach. 2008. *Structured Topic Models for Language*. Ph.D. thesis, University of Cambridge.

Andrew Weir. 2012. Left-edge deletion in english and subject omission in diaries. *English Language and Linguistics*.

Andrew T. Wilson and Peter A. Chew. 2010. Term weighting schemes for latent dirichlet allocation. In *Human Language Technologies: The 2010 Annual Conference of the North American Chapter of the Association for Computational Linguistics*, HLT '10, pages 465–473, Stroudsburg, PA, USA. Association for Computational Linguistics.

The Role of Emotional Stability in Twitter Conversations

Fabio Celli
CLIC-CIMeC
University of Trento
fabio.celli@unitn.it

Luca Rossi
LaRiCA
University of Urbino
luca.rossi@uniurb.it

Abstract

In this paper, we address the issue of how different personalities interact in Twitter. In particular we study users' interactions using one trait of the standard model known as the "Big Five": emotional stability. We collected a corpus of about 200000 Twitter posts and we annotated it with an unsupervised personality recognition system. This system exploits linguistic features, such as punctuation and emoticons, and statistical features, such as followers count and retweeted posts. We tested the system on a dataset annotated with personality models produced from human judgements. Network analysis shows that neurotic users post more than secure ones and have the tendency to build longer chains of interacting users. Secure users instead have more mutual connections and simpler networks.

1 Introduction and Background

Twitter is one of the most popular micro-blogging web services. It was founded in 2006, and allows users to post short messages up to 140 characters of text, called "tweets".

Following the definition in Boyd and Ellison (2007), Twitter is a social network site, but is shares some features with blogs. Zhao and Rosson (2009) highlights the fact that people use twitter for a variety of social purposes like keeping in touch with friends and colleagues, raising the visibility of their interests, gathering useful information, seeking for help and relaxing. They also report that the way people use Twitter can be grouped in three broad classes: people updating personal life activities, people doing real-time information and people following other people's RSS feeds, which is a way to keep informed about personal intersts.

According to Boyd et al. (2010), there are many features that affect practices and conversations in Twitter. First of all, connections in Twitter are directed rather than mutual: users follow other users' feeds and are followed by other users. Public messages can be addressed to specific users with the symbol `@`. According to Honeycutt and Herring (2009) this is used to reply to, to cite or to include someone in a conversation. Messages can be marked and categorized using the "hashtag" symbol `#`, that works as an aggregator of posts having something in common. Another important feature is that posts can be shared and propagated using the "retweet" option. Boyd et al. (2010) emphasize the fact that retweeting a post is a means of participating in a diffuse conversation. Moreover, posts can be marked as favorites and users can be included into lists. Those practices enhance the visibility of the posts or the users.

In recent years the interest towards Twitter raised in the scientific community, especially in Information Retrieval. For example Pak and Paroubek (2010) developed a sentiment analysis classifier from Twitter data, Finin et al. (2010) performed Named Entity Recognition on Twitter using crowdsourcing services such as Mechanical Turk[1] and CrowdFlower[2], and Zhao et al. (2011) proposed a ranking algorithm for extracting topic keyphrases from tweets. Of course also in the personality recog-

[1]https://www.mturk.com/mturk/welcome
[2]http://crowdflower.com

Proceedings of the 13th Conference of the European Chapter of the Association for Computational Linguistics, pages 10–17,
Avignon, France, April 23 - 27 2012. ©2012 Association for Computational Linguistics

nition field there is a great interest towards the analysis of Twitter. For example Quercia et al. (2011) analyzed the correlations between personality traits and the behaviour of four types of users: listeners, popular, hi-read and influential.

In this paper, we describe a personality recognition tool we developed in order to annotate data from Twitter and we analyze how emotional stability affects interactions in Twitter. In the next section, given an overview of personality recognition and emotional stability, we will describe our personality recognition system in detail and we present the dataset we collected from Twitter. In the last two sections we report and discuss the results of the experiment and we provide some provisional conclusions.

2 Personality Recognition

2.1 Definition of Personality and Emotional Stability

Personality is a complex of attributes that characterise a unique individual. Psychologists, see for example Goldberg (1992), formalize personality along five traits known as the "Big Five", a model introduced by Norman (1963) that has become a standard over the years. The five traits are the following: **Extraversion** (sociable vs shy); **Emotional stability** (calm vs insecure); **Agreeableness** (friendly vs uncooperative); **Conscientiousness** (organized vs careless); **Openness** (insightful vs unimaginative).

Among all the 5 traits, emotional stability plays a crucial role in social networks. Studying offline social networks, Kanfer and Tanaka (1993) report that secure (high emotional stability) subjects had more people interacting with them. Moreover, Van Zalk et al. (2011) reports that youths who are socially anxious (low emotional stability) have fewer friends in their network and tend to choose friends who are socially anxious too. We will test if it is true also in online social networks.

2.2 Previous Work and State of the Art

Computational linguistics community started to pay attention to personality recognition only recently. A pioneering work by Argamon et al. (2005) classified neuroticism and extraversion using linguistic features such as function words, deictics, appraisal expressions and modal verbs. Oberlander and Nowson (2006) classified extraversion, emotional stability, agreeableness and conscientiousness of blog authors' using n-grams as features. Mairesse et al. (2007) reported a long list of correlations between big5 personality traits and 2 feature sets, one from linguistics (LIWC, see Pennebaker et al. (2001) for details) and one from psychology (RMC, see Coltheart (1981)). Those sets included features such as punctuation, length and frequency of words used. They obtained those correlations from psychological factor analysis on a corpus of Essays (see Pennebaker and King (1999) for details) annotated with personality, and developed a supervisd system for personality recognition available online as a demo[3]. In a recent work, Iacobelli et al. (2011) tested different feature sets, extracted from a corpus of blogs, and found that bigrams and stop words treated as boolean features yield very good results. As is stated by the authors themselves, their model may overfit the data, since the n-grams extracted are very few in a very large corpus. Quercia et al. (2011) predicted personality scores of Twitter users by means of network statistics like following count and retweet count, but they report root mean squared error, not accuracy. Finally Golbeck et al. (2011) predicted the personality of 279 users from Facebook using either linguistic. such as word and long-word count, and extralinguistic features, such as friend count and the like. The State-of-the-art in personality recognition is reported in table 1. Argamon (Arg05) and Oberlander (Ob06) use naive bayes, Mairesse (Mai07) and Iacobelli (Ia11) use support vector machines and Golbeck (Gol11) uses M5 rules with a mix of linguistic and extralinguistic features.

E.Stab.	**Arg05**	**Ob06**	**Mai07**	**Ia11**	**Gol11**
acc	0.581	0.558	0.573	0.705	0.531

Table 1: State-of-the-Art in Personality Recognition from language for the emotional stability trait.

2.3 Description of the Unsupervised Personality Recognition Tool

Given a set of correlations between personality traits and some linguistic or extralinguistic features, we

[3]http://people.csail.mit.edu/francois/research/personality/demo.html

are able to develop a system that builds models of personality for each user in a social network site whose data are publicly available. In our system personality models can take 3 possible values: secure (s), neurotic (n) and omitted/balanced (o), indicating that a user do not show any feature or shows both the features of a neurotic and a secure user in equal measure. Many scholars provide sets of correlations between some cues and the traits of personality formalized in the big5. In our system we used a feature set taken partly from Mairesse et al. (2007) and partly from Quercia et al. (2011). The former provides a long list of linguistic cues that correlate with personality traits in English. The latter provides the correlations between personality traits and the count of following, followers, listed and retweeted.

We selected the features reported in table 2, since they are the most frequent in the dataset for which we have correlation coefficients with emotional stability.

Features	Corr. to Em. Stab.	from
exclam. marks	-.05*	Mai07
neg. emot.	-.18**	Mai07
numbers	.05*	Mai07
pos. emot.	.07**	Mai07
quest. marks	-.05*	Mai07
long words	.06**	Mai07
w/t freq.	.10**	Mai07
following	-.17**	Qu11
followers	-.19**	Qu11
retweeted	-.03*	Qu11

Table 2: Features used in the system and their Pearson's correlation coefficients with personality traits as reported in Mairesse et al. (2007) and Quercia et al. (2011). * = p smaller than .05 (weak correlation), ** = p smaller than .01 (strong correlation)

Exclamation marks: the count of ! in a post; **negative emoticons**: the count of emoticons expressing negative feelings in a post; **numbers**: the count of numbers in the post; **positive emoticons**: the count of emoticons expressing positive feelings in a post; **question marks**: the count of ? in a post; **long words**: count of words longer than 6 characters in the post; **word/token frequency**: frequency of repeated words in a post, defined as

$$wt = \frac{repeated\ words}{post\ word\ count}$$

following count: the count of users followed; **followers count**: the count of followers; **retweeted count**: the amount of user's posts retweeted.

The processing pipeline, as shown in figure 1, is divided in three steps: preprocess, process and evaluation.

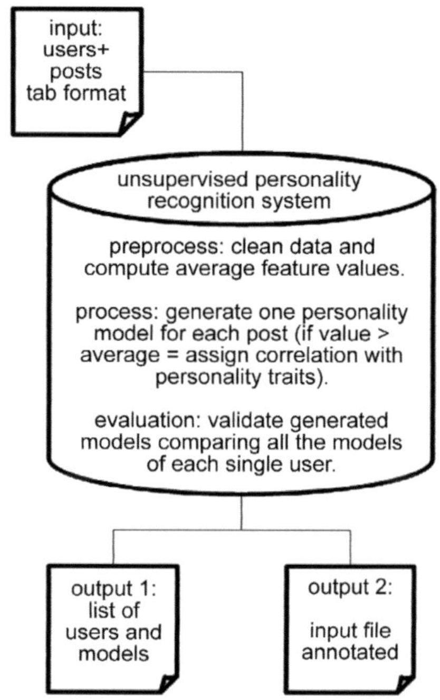

Figure 1: Unsupervised Personality Recognition System pipeline.

In the preprocessing phase the system randomly samples a predefined number of posts (in this case 2000) in order to capture the average occurrence of each feature. In the processing phase the system generates one personality model per post matching features and applying correlations. If the system finds feature values above the average, it increments or decrements the score associated to emotional stability, depending on a positive or negative correlation. The list of all features used and their correlations with personality traits provided by Mairesse et al. (2007) (Mai07) and Quercia et al. (2011) (Qu11), is reported in table 2.

In order to evaluate the personality models generated, the system compares all the models generated for each post of a single user and retrieves one model per user. This is based on the assumption that one user has one and only one complex personality, and that this personality emerges at a various levels from written text, as well as from other extralinguistic cues. The system provides confidence and variability as evaluation measures. Confidence gives a measure of the consistency of the personality model. It is defined as

$$c = \frac{tp}{M}$$

where *tp* is the amount of personality models (for example "s" and"s", "n" and "n"), matching while comparing all posts of a user and *M* is the amount of the models generated for that user. Variability gives information about how much one user tends to write expressing the same personality traits in all the posts. It is defined as

$$v = \frac{c}{P}$$

where *c* is confidence score and *P* is the count of all user's posts. The system can evaluate personality only for users that have more than one post, the other users are discarded.

Our personality recognition system is unsupervised. This means that it exploits correlations in order to build models and does not require previously annotated data to modelize personality. Since the evaluation is performed directly on the dataset we need to test the system before using it. In the following section we describe how we tested system's performance.

2.4 Testing the Unsupervised Personality Recognition Tool

We run two tests, the first one to evaluate the accuracy in predicting human judges on personality, and the second one to evaluate the performance of the system on Twitter data. In the first one, we compared the results of our system on a dataset, called Personage (see Mairesse and Walker (2007)), annotated with personality ratings from human judges. Raters expressed their judgements on a scale from 1 (low) to 7 (high) for each of the Big Five personality traits on English sentences. In order to obtain a gold standard, we converted this scale into our three-values scheme applying the following rules: if value is greater or equal to 5 then we have "s", if value is 4 we have "o" and if value is smaller or equal to 3 we have "n". We used a balanced set of 8 users (20 sentences per user), we generated personality models automatically and we compared them to the gold standard. We obtained an accuracy of 0.625 over a majority baseline of 0.5, which is in line with the state of the art.

In the second test we compared the output of our system to the score of Analyzewords[4], an online tool for Twitter analysis based on LIWC features (see Pennebaker et al. (2001)). This tool does not provide big5 traits but, among others, it returns scores for "worried" and "upbeat", and we used those classes to evaluate "n" and "s" respectively. We randomly extracted 18 users from our dataset (see section 3 for details), 10 neurotics and 8 secure, and we manually checked whether the classes assigned by our system matched the scores of Analyzewords. Results, reported in table 3, reveal that our system has a good precision in detecting worried/neurotic users. The bad results for upbeat/secure users could be due to the fact that the class "upbeat" do not correspond perfectly to the "secure" class. Overall the performance of our system is in line with the state of the art.

	p	r	f1
n	0.8	0.615	0.695
s	0.375	0.6	0.462
avg	0.587	0.607	0.578

Table 3: Results of test 2.

3 Collection of the Dataset

The corpus, called "Personalitwit2", was collected starting from Twitter's public timeline[5]. The sampling procedure is depicted in figure 2.

We sampled data from December 25th to 28th, 2011 but most of the posts have a previous posting date since we also collected data from user pages, where 20 recent tweets are displayed in reverse chronological order. For each public user, sampled from the public timeline, we collected the nicknames of the related users, who had a conversation with the public users, using the @ symbol. We did this in order to capture users that are included in social relationships with the public users.

[4]http://www.analyzewords.com/index.php
[5]http://twitter.com/public timeline

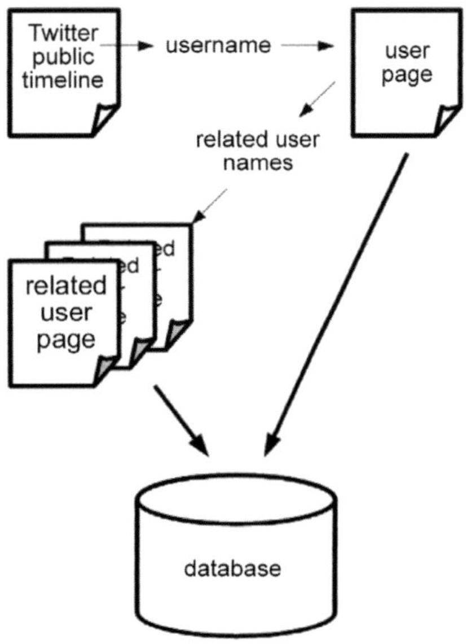

Figure 2: Data sampling pipeline.

We excluded from sampling all the retweeted posts because they are not written by the user themselves and could affect linguistic-based personality recognition. The dataset contains all the following information for each post: username; text; post date; user type (public user or related user); user retweet count; user following count; user followers count; user listed count; user favorites count; total tweet count; user page creation year; time zone; related users (users who replied to the sampled user); reply score (*rp*), defined as

$$rp = \frac{\textit{page reply count}}{\textit{page post count}}$$

and retweet score (*rt*), defined as

$$rt = \frac{\textit{page retweet count}}{\textit{page post count}}$$

	min	**median**	**mean**	**max**
tweets	3	5284	12246	582057
following	0	197	838	320849
followers	0	240	34502	17286123
listed	0	1	385	539019
favorites	0	7	157	62689

Table 4: Summary of Personalitwit2.

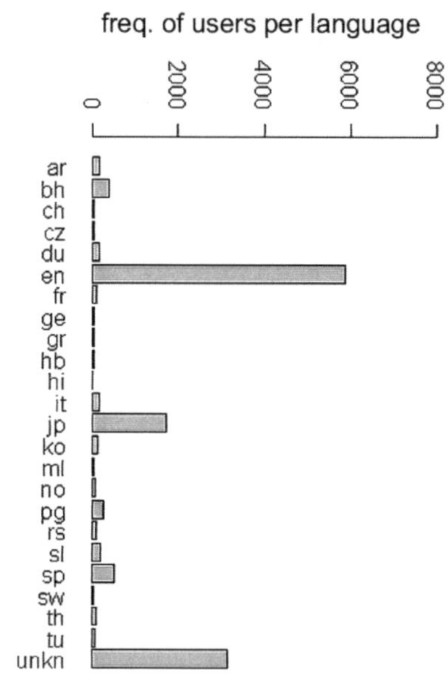

Figure 3: Frequency distribution of users per language. From the top: Arabic, Bahasa, Chinese, Czech, Dutch, English, French, German, Greek, Hebrew, Hindi, Italian, Japanese, Korean, Malay, Norwegian, Portuguese, Russian, Slovene, Spanish, Swedish, Thai, Turkish, Unidentified.

In the corpus there are 200000 posts, more than 13000 different users and about 7800 ego-networks, where public users are the central nodes and related users are the edges. We annotated the corpus with our personality recognition system. The average confidence is 0.601 and the average variability is 0.049. A statistical summary of the data we collected is reported in table 4, the distribution of users per language is reported in figure 3. We kept only English users (5392 egonetworks), discarding all the other users.

4 Experiments and Discussion

Frequency distribution of emotional stability trait in the corpus is as follows: 56.1% calm users, 39.2% neurotic users and 4.7% balanced users.

We run a first experiment to check whether neurotic or calm users tend to have conversations with other users with the same personality trait. To this purpose we extracted all the ego-networks annotated with personality. We automatically extracted

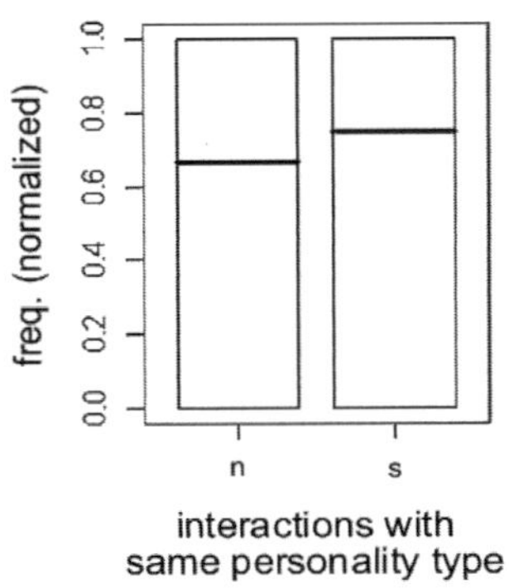

Figure 4: Relationships between users with the same personality traits.

the trait of the personality of the "public-user" (the center of the network) and we counted how many edges of the ego-network have the same personality trait. The users in the ego-network are weighted: this means that if a "public-user" had x conversations with the same "related-user", it is counted x times. The frequency is defined as

$$freq = \frac{trait\ count}{egonetwork\ nodes\ count}$$

where the same trait is between the public-user and the related users. The experiment, whose results are reported in figure 4, shows that there is a general tendency to have conversations between users that share the same traits.

We run a second experiment to find which personality type is most incline to tweet, to retweet and to reply. Results, reported in figure 5, show that neurotic users tend to post and to retweet more than stable users. Stable users are slightly more inclined to reply with respect to neurotic ones.

In order to study if conversational practices among users with similar personality traits might generate different social structure, we applied a social network analysis to the collected data through the use of the Gephi software[6]. We analysed separately the network of interactions between neurotic users (n) and calm users (s) to point out any personality related aspect of the emerging social structure. Visualisations are shown in figure 6.

Due to the way in which data have been acquired

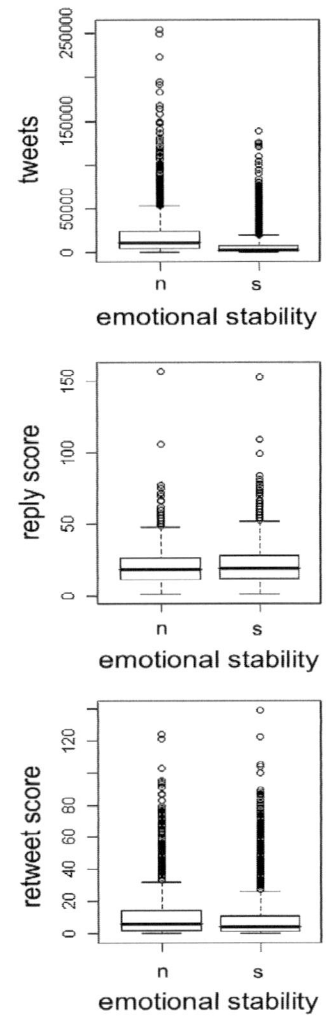

Figure 5: Relationships between emotional stability and Twitter activity.

- starting from the users randomly displayed on the Twitter public timeline - there is a large number of scattered networks made of few interactions. Nevertheless the extraction of the ego networks allowed us to detect a rather interesting phenomena: neurotic users seem to have the tendency to build longer chains of interacting users while calm users have the tendency to build mutual connections.

The average path length value of neurotic users is 1.551, versus the average path length measured on the calm users of 1.334. This difference results in a network diameter of 6 for the network made of only neurotic users and of 5 for the network made

[6]http://www.gephi.org

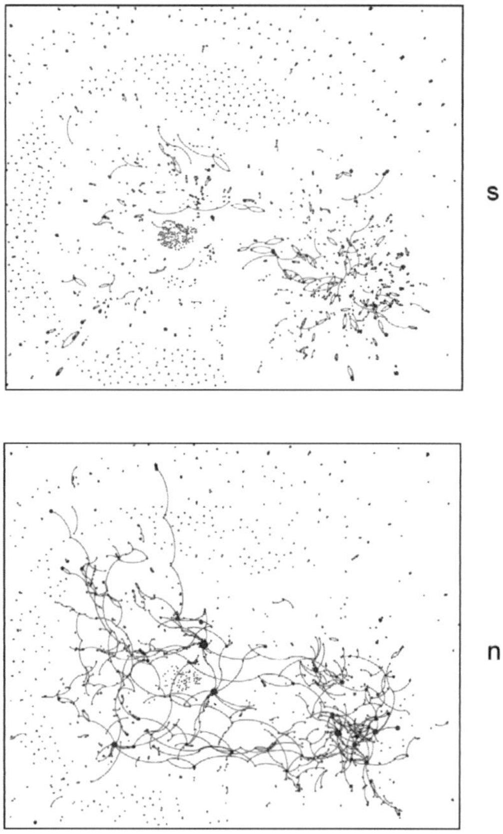

Figure 6: Social structures of stable (s) and neurotic (n) users.

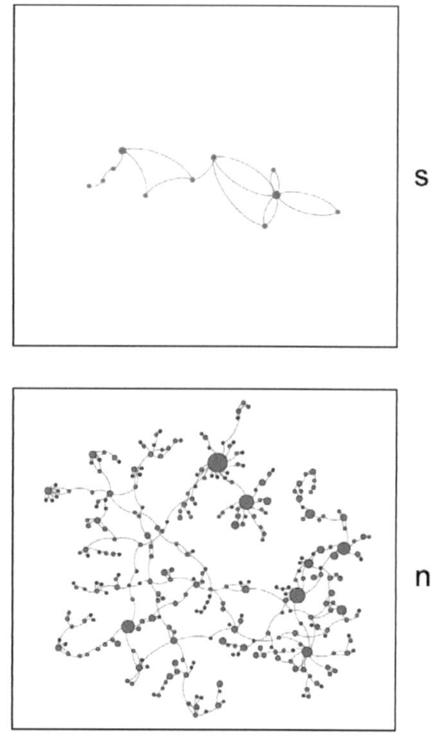

Figure 7: Giant components of stable (s) and neurotic (n) users.

of secure users. A single point of difference in the network diameter produces a neurotic network much more complex than the calm network. While this difference might be overlooked in large visualisations due to the presence of many minor clusters of nodes it becomes evident when we focus only on the giant component of the two networks in figure 7.

The giant components are those counting the major part of nodes and can be used as an example of the most complex structure existing within a network. As it should appear clear neurotic network contains more complex interconnected structures than calm network even if, as we claimed before, have on average smaller social networks.

5 Conclusions and Future Work

In this paper, we presented an unsupervised system for personality recognition and we applied it successfully on a quite large and richly annotated Twitter dataset. Results confirm some offline psychological findings in the social networks online, for example the fact that neurotic people tend to choose friends who are also neurotic.

We also confirm the fact that neurotic users have smaller social networks at the level of a single user, but they tend to build longer chains. This means that a tweet propagated in "neurotic networks" has higher visibility. We also found that neurotic users have the highest posting rate and retweet score.

In the future we should change the sampling settings in order to capture larger networks. It would be also very interesting to explore how other personality traits affect user's behaviour. To this purpose we need to improve the personality recognition system and we would benefit from topic identification, which is another growing field of research.

References

Amichai-Hamburger, Y. and Vinitzky, G. 2010. Social network use and personality. In *Computers in Human Behavior*. 26(6). pp. 1289–1295.

Argamon, S., Dhawle S., Koppel, M., Pennebaker J. W. 2005. Lexical Predictors of Personality Type. In *Proceedings of Joint Annual Meeting of the Interface and the Classification Society of North America*. pp. 1–16.

Bastian M., Heymann S., Jacomy M. 2009. Gephi: an open source software for exploring and manipulating networks. In *Proceedings of International AAAI Conference on Weblogs and Social Media*. pp. 1–2.

Boyd, D. Golder, S. and Lotan, G. 2010. Tweet, Tweet, Retweet: Conversational Aspects of Retweeting on Twitter. In *Proceedings of HICSS-43*. pp. 1–10.

Boyd, D. and Ellison, N. 2007. Social Network Sites: Definition, history, and scholarship. In *Journal of Computer-Mediated Communication* 13(1). pp. 210–230.

Celli, F., Di Lascio F.M.L., Magnani, M., Pacelli, B., and Rossi, L. 2010. *Social Network Data and Practices: the case of Friendfeed*. Advances in Social Computing, pp. 346–353. Series: Lecture Notes in Computer Science, Springer, Berlin.

Coltheart, M. 1981. The MRC psycholinguistic database. In *Quarterly Journal of Experimental Psychology*, 33A, pp. 497–505.

Finin, T., Murnane, W., Karandikar, A., Keller, N., Martineau, J., Dredze, M. 2010. Annotating named entities in Twitter data with crowdsourcing. In *Proceedings of the NAACL HLT 2010 Workshop on Creating Speech and Language Data with Amazon's Mechanical Turk (CSLDAMT '10)*. pp. 80–88.

Golbeck, J. and Robles, C., and Turner, K. 2011. Predicting Personality with Social Media. In *Proceedings of the 2011 annual conference extended abstracts on Human factors in computing systems*, pp. 253–262.

Golbeck, J. and Hansen, D.,L. 2011. Computing political preference among twitter followers. In *Proceedings of CHI 2011*: pp. 1105–1108.

Goldberg, L., R. The Development of Markers for the Big Five factor Structure. 1992. In *Psychological Assessment*, 4(1). pp. 26–42.

Honeycutt, C., and Herring, S. C. 2009. Beyond microblogging: Conversation and collaboration via Twitter. In *Proceedings of the Forty-Second Hawaii International Conference on System Sciences*. pp 1–10.

Kanfer, A., Tanaka, J.S. 1993. *Unraveling the Web of Personality Judgments: The Inuence of Social Networks on Personality Assessment*. Journal of Personality, 61(4) pp. 711–738.

Iacobelli, F., Gill, A.J., Nowson, S. Oberlander, J. Large scale personality classification of bloggers. 2011. In *Lecture Notes in Computer Science (6975)*, pp. 568–577.

Mairesse, F., and Walker, M.. PERSONAGE: Personality Generation for Dialogue. 2007. In *Proceedings of the 45th Annual Meeting of the Association for Computational Linguistics (ACL)*, pp.496–503.

Mairesse, F. and Walker, M. A. and Mehl, M. R., and Moore, R, K. 2007. Using Linguistic Cues for the Automatic Recognition of Personality in Conversation and Text. In *Journal of Artificial intelligence Research*, 30. pp. 457–500.

Norman, W., T. 1963. Toward an adequate taxonomy of personality attributes: Replicated factor structure in peer nomination personality rating. In *Journal of Abnormal and Social Psychology*, 66. pp. 574–583.

Oberlander, J., and Nowson, S. 2006. Whose thumb is it anyway? classifying author personality from weblog text. In *Proceedings of the 44th Annual Meeting of the Association for Computational Linguistics ACL*. pp. 627–634.

Pak, A., Paroubek P. 2010. Twitter as a corpus for sentiment analysis and opinion mining. In *Proceedings of LREC 2010*. pp. 1320–1326.

Pennebaker, J. W., King, L. A. 1999. Linguistic styles: Language use as an individual difference. In *Journal of Personality and Social Psychology*, 77, pp. 1296–1312.

Pennebaker, J. W., Francis, M. E., Booth, R. J. 2001. *Inquiry and Word Count: LIWC 2001*. Lawrence Erlbaum, Mahwah, NJ.

Platt, J. 1998. Machines using Sequential Minimal Optimization. In Schoelkopf, B., Burges, C., Smola, A. (ed), *Advances in Kernel Methods, Support Vector Learning*. pp. 37–49.

Quercia, D. and Kosinski, M. and Stillwell, D., and Crowcroft, J. 2011. Our Twitter Profiles, Our Selves: Predicting Personality with Twitter. In *Proceedings of SocialCom2011*. pp. 180–185.

Van Zalk, N., Van Zalk, M., Kerr, M. and Stattin, H. 2011. Social Anxiety as a Basis for Friendship Selection and Socialization in Adolescents' Social Networks. Journal of Personality, 79: pp. 499–526.

Zhao, D., Rosson, M.B. 2009. How and why people Twitter: The role that micro-blogging plays in informal communication at work. In *Proceedings of GROUP 2009* pp. 243–252.

Zhao, W.X., Jiang, J., He, J., Song, Y., Achananuparp, P., Lim, E.P., Li, X. 2011. Topical keyphrase extraction from Twitter. In *Proceedings of the 49th Annual Meeting of the Association for Computational Linguistics: Human Language Technologies - Volume 1 (HLT '11)*. pp. 379–388.

Towards Scalable Speech Act Recognition in Twitter: Tackling Insufficient Training Data

Renxian Zhang **Dehong Gao** **Wenjie Li**
Department of Computing
The Hong Kong Polytechnic University
{csrzhang, csdgao, cswjli}@comp.polyu.edu.hk

Abstract

Recognizing speech act types in Twitter is of much theoretical interest and practical use. Our previous research did not adequately address the deficiency of training data for this multi-class learning task. In this work, we set out by assuming only a small seed training set and experiment with two semi-supervised learning schemes, transductive SVM and graph-based label propagation, which can leverage the knowledge about unlabeled data. The efficacy of semi-supervised learning is established by our extensive experiments, which also show that transductive SVM is more suitable than graph-based label propagation for our task. The empirical findings and detailed evidences can contribute to scalable speech act recognition in Twitter.

1. Introduction

The social media platform of Twitter makes available a plethora of data to probe the communicative act of people in a social network woven by interesting events, people, topics, etc. Communicative acts such as disseminating information, asking questions, or expressing feelings all fall in the purview of "speech act", a long established area in pragmatics (Austin 1962). The automatic recognition of speech act in tons of tweets has both theoretical and practical appeal. Practically, it helps tweeters to find topics to read or tweet about based on speech act compositions. Theoretically, it introduces a new dimension to study social media content as well as providing real-life data to validate or falsify claims in the speech act theory.

Different taxonomies of speech act have been proposed by linguists and computational linguists, ranging from a few to over a hundred types. In this work, we adopt the 5 types of speech act used in our previous work (Zhang et al. 2011), which are in turn inherited from (Searle 1975): **statement**, **question**, **suggestion**, **comment**, and **miscellaneous**. Our choice is based on the fact that unlike face-to-face communication, twittering is more in a "broadcasting" style than on a personal basis. Statement and comment, which are usually intended to make one's knowledge, thought, and sentiment known, thus befit Twitter's communicative style. Question and suggestion on Twitter are usually targeted at other tweeters in general or one's followers. More interpersonal speech acts such as "threat" or "thank" as well as rare speech acts in Twitter (Searle's (1975) "commissives" and "declaratives") are relegated to "miscellaneous". Some examples from our experimental datasets are provided in Table 1.

Proceedings of the 13th Conference of the European Chapter of the Association for Computational Linguistics, pages 18–27, Avignon, France, April 23 - 27 2012. ©2012 Association for Computational Linguistics

Tweet	*Speech Act*
Libya Releases 4 Times Journalists - http://www.photozz.com/?104k	**Statement**
#sincewebeinghonest why u so obsessed with what me n her do?? Don't u got ya own man???? Oh wait.....	**Question**
RT @NaonkaMixon: I will donate 10 $ to the Red Cross Japan Earthquake fund for every person that retweets this! #PRAYFORJAPAN	**Suggestion**
is enjoying this new season of #CelebrityApprentice.... Nikki Taylor = Yum!!	**Comment**
65. I want to get married to someone i meet in highschool. #100factsaboutme	**Miscellaneous**

Table 1. Example Tweets with Speech acts

Assuming one tweet demonstrates only one speech act, the automatic recognition of those speech act types in Twitter is a multi-class classification task. We concede that this assumption may not always hold in real situations. But given the short length of tweets, multi-speech act tweets are rare and we find this simplifying assumption effective in reducing the complexity of our problem. A major problem with this task is the deficiency of training data. Tweeters as well as face-to-face interlocutors do not often identify their speech acts; human annotation is costly and time-consuming. Although our previous research (Zhang et al. 2011) sheds light on the preparation of training data, it did not adequately address this problem.

Our contribution in this work is to directly address the problem of training data deficiency by using two well-known semi-supervised learning techniques that leverage the relationship between a small seed of training data and a large body of unlabeled data: transductive SVM and graph-based label propagation. The empirical results show that the knowledge about unlabeled data provides promising solutions to the data deficiency problem, and that transductive SVM is more competent for our task. Our exploration with different training/unlabeled data ratios for three major Twitter categories and a mixed-type category provides solid evidential support for future research.

The rest of the paper is organized as follows. Section 2 reviews works related to speech act recognition and semi-supervised learning; Section 3 briefly discusses supervised learning of speech act types developed in our earlier work and complementing the previous findings with learning curves. The technical details of semi-supervised learning are presented in Section 4. Then we report and discuss the results of our experiments in Section 5. Finally, Section 6 concludes the paper and outlines future directions.

2. Related Work

The automatic recognition of speech act, also known as "dialogue act", has attracted sustained interest in computational linguistics and speech technology for over a decade (Searle 1975; Stolcke et al. 2000). A few annotated corpora such as Switchboard-DAMSL (Jurafsky et al. 1997) and Meeting Recorder Dialog Act (Dhillon et al. 2004) are widely used, with data transcribed from telephone or face-to-face conversation.

Prior to the flourish of microblogging services such as Twitter, speech act recognition has been extended to electronic media such as email and discussion forum (Cohen et al. 2004; Feng et al. 2006) in order to study the behavior of email or message senders.

The annotated corpora for ordinary verbal communications and the methods developed for email, or discussion forum cannot be directly used for our task because Twitter text has a distinctive Netspeak style that is situated between speech and text but resembles neither (Crystal 2006, 2011). Compared with email or forum post, it is rife with linguistic noises such as spelling mistakes, random coinages, mixed use of letters and symbols.

Speech act recognition in Twitter is a fairly new task. In our pioneering work (Zhang et al. 2011), we show that Twitter text normalization is unnecessary and even counterproductive for this task. More importantly, we propose a set of useful features and draw empirical conclusion about the scope of this task, such as recognizing speech act on the coarse-grade category level works as well as on the fine-grade topic level. In this work, we continue to adopt this framework including other learning details (speech act types and feature selection for tweets), but the new quest starts where the old one left: tackling insufficient training data.

As in many practical applications, sufficient annotated data are hard to obtain. Therefore, unsupervised and semi-supervised learning methods are actively pursued. While unsupervised sentence classification is rule-based and domain-dependent (Deshpande et al. 2010), semi-supervised methods that both alleviate the data deficiency problem and leverage the power of state-of-the-art classifiers hold more promises for different domains (Medlock and Briscoe 2007; Erkan et al. 2007).

In the machine learning literature, a classic semi-supervised learning scheme is proposed by Yarowsky (1995), which is a classical self-teaching process that makes no use of labeled data before they are classified. More theoretical analyses are made by (Culp and Michailidis 2007) and (Haffari and Sarkar 2007).

Transductive SVM (Joachims 1999) extends the state-of-the-art inductive SVM by explicitly considering the relationship between labeled and unlabeled data. The graph-based label propagation model (Zhu et al. 2003; Zhou et al. 2004) using a harmonic function also accommodates the knowledge about unlabeled data. We will adapt both of them to our multi-class classification task.

Jeong et al. (2009) report a semi-supervised approach to classifying speech acts in emails and online forums. But their subtree-based method is not applicable to our task because Twitter's noisy textual quality cannot be found in the much cleaner email or forum texts.

3. Supervised Learning of Speech Act Types

Supervised learning of speech act types in Twitter relies heavily on a good set of features that capture the textual characteristics of both Twitter and speech act utterances. As in our previous work, we use speech act-specific cues, special words (abbreviations and acronyms, opinion words, vulgar words, and emoticons), and special characters (Twitter-specific characters and a few punctuations). Tweet-external features such as tweeter profile may also help, but that is beyond the focus of this paper.

Although it has been empirically shown that speech act recognition in Twitter can be done without using training data specific to topics or even categories, it is not clear how much training data is needed to achieve desirable performance. In order to answer this question, we adopt the same experimental setup and datasets as reported in (Zhang et al. 2011) and plot the learning curves shown in Figure 1.

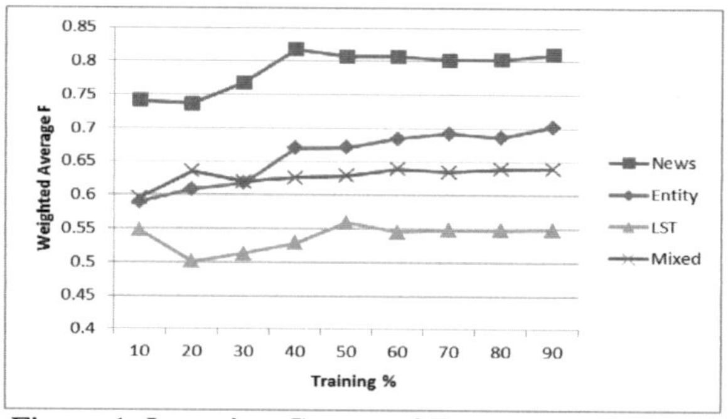

Figure 1. Learning Curves of Each Category and All Tweets

For all individual experiments, the test data are a randomly sampled 10% set of all annotated data. When training data reach 90%, we actually duplicate the reported results. However, Figure 1 shows that it is unnecessary to use so much training data to achieve good classification performance. For News and Entity, the classification makes little noticeable improvement after the training data ratio reaches 40% (training : test = 4 : 1). For Mixed (the aggregate of the News, Entity, LST datasets) and LST, performance peaks even earlier at 20% training data (training : test = 2 : 1) and 10% (training : test = 1 : 1).

It is delightful to see that only a moderate number of annotated data are needed for speech act recognition. But even that number (for the Mixed dataset, 10% training data are over 800 annotated tweets) may not be available and in many situations, test data may be much more than training data. Taking this challenge is the next important step we make.

4. Semi-Supervised Learning of Speech Act Types

The problem setting of a small seed training (labeled) set and a much larger test (labeled) set fits the semi-supervised learning scheme. Classic semi-supervised learning approaches such as self-teaching methods (e.g., Yarowsky 1995) are mainly concerned with incrementing high-confidence labeled data in each round of training. They do not, however, directly take into account the knowledge about unlabeled data. The recent research emphasis is on leveraging knowledge about unlabeled data during training. In this section, we discuss two such approaches.

4.1 Transductive SVM

The standard SVM classifier popularly used in text classification is also known as inductive SVM as a model is induced from training data. The model is solely dependent on the training data and agnostic about the test data. In contrast, transductive SVM (Vapnik 1998; Joachims 1999) predicts test labels by using the knowledge about test data. In the case of test (unlabeled) data far outnumbering training (labeled) data, transductive SVM provides a feasible scheme of semi-supervised learning.

For a single-class classification problem $\{\mathbf{x}_i, y_i\}$ that focuses on only one speech act type, where $\mathbf{x}_i$ is the ith tweet and y_i is the corresponding label and $y_i \in \{+1, -1\}$ denotes whether $\mathbf{x}_i$ contains the speech act or not, inductive SVM is formulated to find an optimal hyperplane $sign(\mathbf{w}\cdot\mathbf{x}_i - b)$ to maximize the soft margin between positive and negative objects, or to minimize:

$$1/2\|\mathbf{w}\|^2 + C\sum_i \phi_i$$

$$\text{s.t. } y_i(\mathbf{x}_i \cdot \mathbf{w} - b) \geq 1 - \phi_i,\ \phi_i \geq 0$$

where ϕ_i is a slack variable. Adopting the same formulation, transductive SVM further considers test data $\mathbf{x}_i$* during training by finding a labeling y_j* and a hyperplane to maximize the soft margin between both training and test data, or to minimize:

$$1/2\|\mathbf{w}\|^2 + C_1\sum_i \phi_i + C_2\sum_i \varphi_i$$

$$\text{s.t. } y_i(\mathbf{x}_i \cdot \mathbf{w} - b) \geq 1 - \phi_i,\ \phi_i \geq 0$$

$$y_i^*(\mathbf{x}_i^* \cdot \mathbf{w} - b) \geq 1 - \varphi_i,\ \varphi_i \geq 0$$

where φ_i is a slack variable for the test data. In fact, labeling test data is done during training.

As the maximal margin approach proves very effective for text classification, its transductive variant that effectively uses the knowledge about test data holds promises of handling the deficiency of labeled data.

4.2 Graph-based Label Propagation

An alternative way of using unlabeled data in semi-supervised learning is based on the intuition that similar objects should belong to the same class, which can be translated into label smoothness on a graph with weights indicating object similarities. This is the idea underlying Zhu et al.'s (2003) graph-based label propagation model using Gaussian random fields.

We again focus on a single-class classification problem. Formally, $\{\mathbf{x}_1, \dots \mathbf{x}_N\}$ are N tweets, having their actual speech act labels $\mathbf{y} = \{y_1, \dots y_L, \dots y_N\}$ ($y_i \in \{1, 0\}$ denoting whether $\mathbf{x}_i$ contains the speech act or not) with the first L of them known, and $\mathbf{f} = \{f_1, \dots f_L, \dots f_N\}$ are their predicted labels. Let $L = \{\mathbf{x}_1, \dots \mathbf{x}_L\}$ and $U = \{\mathbf{x}_{L+1}, \dots \mathbf{x}_N\}$ and the task is to determine $\{f_{L+1}, \dots f_N\}$ for U. We further define a graph $G = (V, E)$, where $V = L \cup U$ and E is weighted by $\mathbf{W} = [w_{ij}]_{N\times N}$ with w_{ij} denoting the similarity between $\mathbf{x}_i$ and $\mathbf{x}_j$. Preferring label smoothness on G and preserving the given labels, we want to minimize the loss function:

$$E(\mathbf{f}) = 1/2 \sum_{i,j\in L\cup U} w_{ij}(f_i - f_j)^2 = \mathbf{f}^T \boldsymbol{\Delta} \mathbf{f}$$

$$\text{s.t. } f_i = y_i\ (i = 1, \dots, L)$$

where $\boldsymbol{\Delta} = \mathbf{D} - \mathbf{W}$ is the combinatorial graph Laplacian with $\mathbf{D}$ being a diagonal matrix $[d_{ij}]_{N\times N}$ and $d_{ii} = \sum_j w_{ij}$.

This can be expressed as a harmonic function, $h = \text{argmin}_{f_L = y_L} E(\mathbf{f})$, which satisfies the smoothness property on the graph: $h(i) = 1/d_{ii}\sum_k w_{ik}(h(k))$. If we define $p_{ij} = w_{ij} / \sum_k w_{ik}$ and collect p_{ij} and $h(i)$ into matrix $\mathbf{P}$ and column vector $\mathbf{h}$, solving $\Delta h = 0$ s.t. $\mathbf{h}_L = \mathbf{y}_L$ is equivalent to solving $\mathbf{h} = \mathbf{Ph}$.

To find the solution, we can use L and U to partition $\mathbf{h}$ and $\mathbf{P}$:

$$\mathbf{h} = \begin{bmatrix} \mathbf{h}_L \\ \mathbf{h}_U \end{bmatrix}, \mathbf{P} = \begin{bmatrix} \mathbf{P}_{LL}, \mathbf{P}_{LU} \\ \mathbf{P}_{UL}, \mathbf{P}_{UU} \end{bmatrix}$$

and it can be shown that $\mathbf{h}_U = (\mathbf{I} - \mathbf{P}_{UU})^{-1}\mathbf{P}_{UL}\mathbf{y}_L$. To get the final classification result, those elements in $\mathbf{h}_U$ that are greater than a threshold (0.5) become 1 and the others become 0.

This approach propagates labels from labeled data to unlabeled data on the principle of label smoothness. If the assumption about similar tweets having same speech acts holds, it should work well for our problem.

4.3 Multi-class Classification

In the previous formulations, we emphasized "single-class classification" because both transductive SVM and graph-based label propagation are inherently one class-oriented. Since our problem is a multi-class one, we transform the problem to single-class classifications by using the one-vs-all scheme.

Specifically, for each class (speech act type) c_i, we label all training instances belonging to c_i as $+1$ and all those belonging to other classes as -1 and then do binary classification. For our problem with 5 speech act types, we make 5 such transformations. The final prediction is made by choosing the class with the highest classification score from the 5 binary classifiers. Both transductive SVM and graph-based label propagation produce real-valued classification scores and are amenable to this scheme.

5. Experiments

Our experiments are designed to answer two questions: 1) How useful is semi-supervised speech act learning in comparison with supervised learning? 2) Which semi-supervised learning approach is more appropriate for our problem?

5.1 Experimental Setup

We use the 6 datasets in our previous study[1], which fall into 3 categories: *News*, *Entity*, *Long-standing Topic* (*LST*). Each of the total 8613 tweets is labeled with one of the following speech act types: *sta* (statement), *que* (question), *sug* (suggestion), *com* (comment), *mis* (miscellaneous). In addition, we randomly select 1000 tweets from each of the categories to create a *Mixed* category of 3000 tweets. Figures 2 to 5 illustrate the distributions of the speech act types in the 3 original categories and the *Mixed* category.

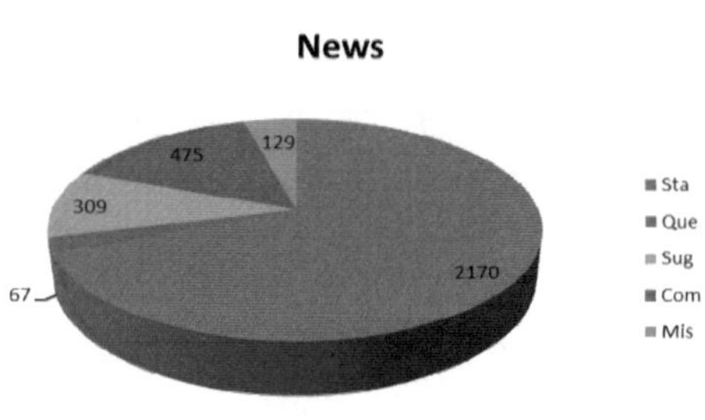

Figure 2. Speech Act Distribution (News)

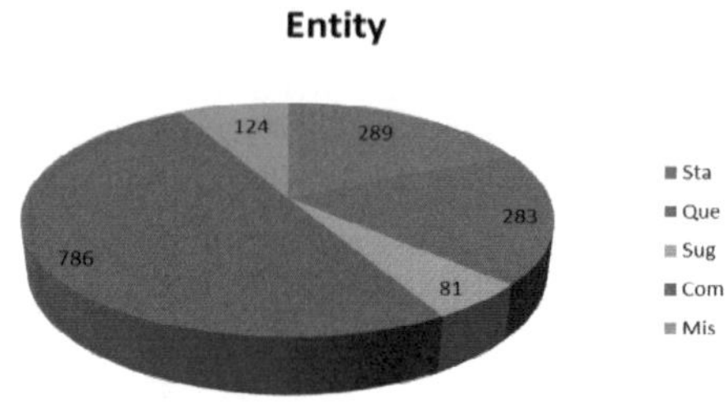

Figure 3. Speech Act Distribution (Entity)

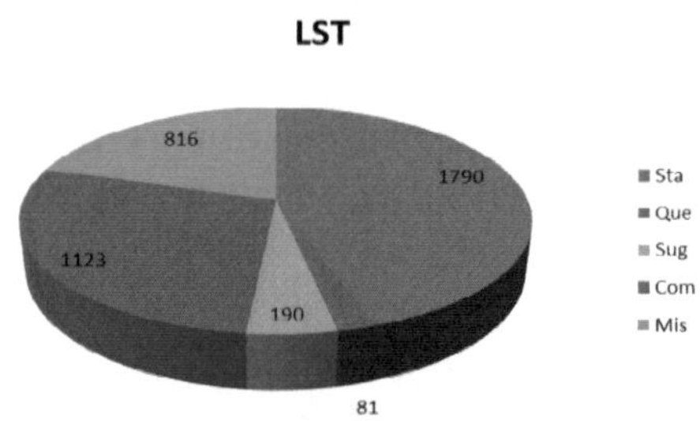

Figure 4. Speech Act Distribution (LST)

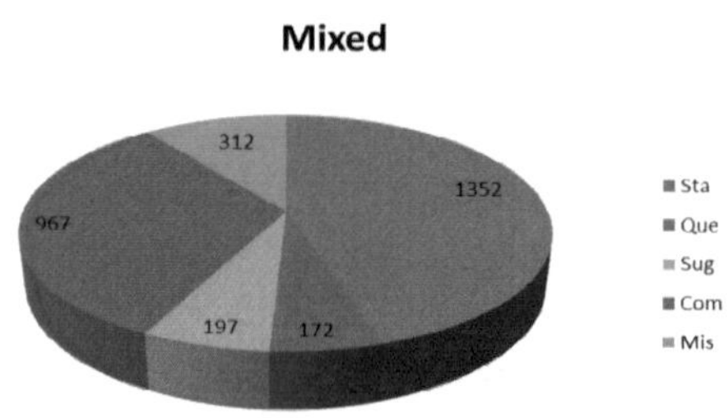

Figure 5. Speech Act Distribution (Mixed)

For each category, we use two labeled/unlabeled data settings, with labeled data accounting for 5% and 10% of the total so that the labeled/unlabeled ratios are set at approximately 1:19 and 1:9. The labeled data in each category are randomly selected in a stratified way: using the same percentage to select labeled data with each speech act type. The stratified selection is intended to keep the speech act distributions in both labeled and unlabeled data. Table 2 and Table 3 list the details of data splitting using the two settings.

Category	# Labeled	# Unlabeled	Total
News	155	2995	3150
Entity	72	1391	1463
LST	198	3802	4000
Mixed	147	2853	3000

Table 2. Stratified Data Splitting with 5% as Labeled

[1] http://www4.comp.polyu.edu.hk/~csrzhang

Category	# Labeled	# Unlabeled	Total
News	312	2838	3150
Entity	144	1319	1463
LST	399	3601	4000
Mixed	298	2702	3000

Table 3. Stratified Data Splitting with 10% as Labeled

For comparison with supervised learning, we also use inductive SVM. The inductive and transductive SVM classifications are implemented by using the SVM^{light} tool[2] with a linear kernel. For the graph-based label propagation method, we populate the similarity matrix **W** with weights calculated by a Gaussian function. Given two tweets $\mathbf{x}_i$ and $\mathbf{x}_j$,

$$w_{ij} = \exp\left(-\frac{\left\|\mathbf{x}_i - \mathbf{x}_j\right\|^2}{2\sigma^2}\right)$$

where $\|.\|$ is the L2 norm. Empirically, the Gaussian function measure leads to better results than other measures such as cosine. Then we convert the graph to an *εNN* graph (Zhu and Goldberg 2009) by removing edges with weight less than a threshold because the *εNN* graph empirically outperforms the fully connected graph. The threshold is set to be $\mu + \sigma$, the mean of all weights plus one standard deviation.

5.2 Results

To better evaluate the performance of semi-supervised learning on speech act recognition in Twitter, we report the classification scores for both multi-class and individual classes, as well as confusion matrices.

Multi-class Evaluation

Table 4 lists the macro-average F scores and weighted average F scores for all classifiers and all categories at the 5% labeled data setting. Macro-average F is chosen because it gives equal weight to all classes. Since some classes (e.g., sta) have much more instances than others (e.g., que), macro-average F ensures that significant score change on minority classes will not be overshadowed by small score change on majority classes. In contrast, weighted average F is calculated according to class instance numbers, which is chosen mainly because we want to compare the result with supervised learning (reported in Zhang et al. 2011 and Figure 1). In this and the following tables, iSVM, tSVM, and GLP denote inductive SVM, transductive SVM, and graph-based label propagation.

	Macro-average F			Weighted average F		
	iSVM	*tSVM*	*GLP*	*iSVM*	*tSVM*	*GLP*
News	.374	.502	.285	.702	.759	.643
Entity	.312	.395	.329	.493	.534	.436
LST	.295	.360	.216	.433	.501	.376
Mixed	.383	.424	.245	.539	.537	.391

Table 4. Multi-class F scores (5% labeled data)

Almost without exception, transductive SVM achieves the best performance. Measured by macro-average F, it outperforms inductive SVM with a gain of 10.7% (Mixed) to 34.2% (News). Consistent with supervised learning results, semi-supervised learning results degrade with News > Entity > LST, indicating that both semi-supervised learning and supervised learning are sensitive to dataset characteristics. More uniform tweet set (e.g., News) leads to better classification and greater improvement by semi-supervised learning. That also explains why the Mixed category, composed of the most diversified tweets, benefits least from semi-supervised learning.

Conversely, supervised learning (inductive SVM) on the Mixed category benefits from the data hodgepodge even though the test data are 19 times the training data. Its macro-average F is higher than the other categories although it does not have the most training data. Its weighted-average F using inductive SVM is even higher than using transductive SVM.

It is a little surprising to find that the graph-based label propagation performs very poorly. In all but one place, the GLP score is lower than its iSVM counterpart. This may indicate that the graph method cannot adapt well to the multi-class scenario and we will show more evidences in the next two sections.

To understand the effectiveness of semi-supervised learning, a better way than doing numerical calculation is juxtaposing semi-supervised data settings with their comparable supervised data settings, which is shown in Table 5. The supervised data settings are of those with the closest weighted average F (waF) to the semi-supervised (tSVM) waF from our previous results (Figure 1).

[2] http://svmlight.joachims.org/

	# labeled	labeled :unlabeled	waF
	Semi-supervised (tSVM)		
News	155	1 : 19	.759
Entity	72	1 : 19	.534
LST	198	1 : 19	.501
Mixed	147	1 : 19	.537
	Supervised (with closest waF)		
News	945	1 : 0.3	.768
Entity	146	1 : 1	.589
LST	800	1 : 0.5	.501
Mixed	861	1 : 1	.596

Table 5. Semi-supervised Learning vs. Supervised Learning

Obviously semi-supervised learning by transductive SVM can achieve classification performance comparable to supervised learning by inductive SVM, with less training data and much lower labeled/unlabeled ratio. This shows that semi-supervised learning such as transductive SVM holds much promise for scalable speech act recognition in Twitter.

It is tempting to think that with more labeled data and higher labeled/unlabeled ratio, semi-supervised learning performance should improve. To put this conjecture to test, we double the labeled data (from 5% to 10%) and labeled/unlabeled ratio (from 1/19 to 1/9), with results in Table 6.

	Macro-average F			**Weighted average F**		
	iSVM	*tSVM*	*GLP*	*iSVM*	*tSVM*	*GLP*
News	.403	.524	.298	.731	.762	.647
Entity	.441	.440	.311	.587	.575	.406
LST	.335	.397	.216	.459	.512	.384
Mixed	.435	.463	.284	.557	.553	.415

Table 6. Multi-class F scores (10% labeled data)

Compared with Table 4, increased labeled data does lead to some improvement, but not much as we would expect, the largest gain being 15.9% (macro-average F on Mixed, using GLP). Note that this is achieved at the cost of labeling twice as much data and predicting half as much. In contrast, the inductive SVM performance is improved by as much as 41.3% (macro-average F on Entity). Such evidence shows that semi-supervised learning of speech acts in Twitter benefits disproportionately little from increased labeled data, or at least the gain is not worth the pain. In fact, this is good news for scalable speech act recognition.

Individual Class Evaluation

For more microscopic inspection, we also report the classification results on individual classes for all categories. In Table 7, we list the rankings of F measures by each classifier for each speech act type and each category. The one-letter notations *i*, *t*, *g* are short for iSVM, tSVM, and GLP. Therefore, $t > g > i$ means tSVM outperforms GLP, which outperforms iSVM, in terms of F measure. The labeled data are 5%.

	Sta	**Que**	**Sug**	**Com**	**Mis**
News	$t>g>i$	$t>i>g$	$t>i>g$	$t>i>g$	$t>g>i$
Entity	$t>g>i$	$t>i>g$	$g>t>i$	$i>t>g$	$t>g>i$
LST	$i>g>t$	$t>i>g$	$i>t>g$	$t>i>g$	$t>g>i$
Mixed	$i>t>g$	$t>i>g$	$t>i>g$	$i>t>g$	$t>g>i$

Table 7. Classifier Rankings for Each Speech Act Type and Category (5% Labeled Data)

In 15 out of the 20 rankings, transductive SVM or graph-based label propagation beats inductive SVM, which shows the efficacy of semi-supervised learning in this class-based perspective. Transductive SVM is the champion, claiming 14 top places.

We also find that the overall performance of graph-based label propagation is the poorest, claiming 12 out of 20 bottom places. After inspecting the data, we observe that the underlying assumption of GLP that similar objects belong to the same class is questionable for speech act recognition in Twitter. Tweets with different speech acts (e.g., question and comment) may appear very similar on the graph. The maximal margin approach is apparently more appropriate for our problem.

On the other hand, the GLP performance evaluated on individual classes is better than evaluated on the multi-class if we compare Table 7 and Table 4, where GLP is almost always the lowest achiever. This indicates that in multi-class classification, GLP suffers further from the one-vs-all converting scheme, a point we will make clearer in the following.

Confusion matrices

Confusion matrix provides another perspective to understand the multi-class classification performance. For brevity's sake, we present the confusion matrices of the three classifiers on the News category with 5% labeled data in Figure 6 to Figure 8. Similar patterns are also observed for the other categories and with 10% labeled data. Note that the rows represent true classes and the columns represent predicted classes.

	Sta	Que	Sug	Com	Mis
Sta	2043	0	5	14	0
Que	46	7	2	9	0
Sug	211	1	61	21	0
Com	276	2	10	164	0
Mis	120	0	1	2	0

Figure 6. Confusion Matrix of iSVM (News, 5% Labeled Data)

	Sta	Que	Sug	Com	Mis
Sta	1848	4	56	90	64
Que	19	17	7	20	1
Sug	95	0	158	31	10
Com	143	5	19	275	10
Mis	94	3	4	15	7

Figure 7. Confusion Matrix of tSVM (News, 5% Labeled Data)

	Sta	Que	Sug	Com	Mis
Sta	1852	0	4	11	195
Que	19	6	0	0	39
Sug	123	0	25	2	144
Com	134	0	0	47	271
Mis	102	0	0	1	20

Figure 8. Confusion Matrix of GLP (News, 5% Labeled Data)

The News category is typically biased towards the statement speech act, which accounts for 69% of the total tweets according to Figure 2. As a result, the iSVM tends to classify tweets of the other speech acts as statement. Figure 6 also shows that the prediction accuracy is correlated with the training amount. The two classes with the least training data, question and miscellaneous, demonstrate the lowest accuracy. Clearly, supervised learning suffers from training data deficiency.

Both tSVM and GLP show the effect of leveraging unlabeled data as they assign new labels to some instances wrongly classified as statement. Transductive SVM is more successful in that it moves most of the Sug and Com instances to the diagonal. The situation for Que and Mis is also better, though the prediction accuracy still suffers from lack of training data. Figure 8, however, reveals an intrinsic problem of applying graph-based label propagation to multi-class classification. Most instances are predicted as either Sta or Mis. The wrong prediction as Mis cannot be explained by imbalance of training data. Rather, it is due to the fact that the single-class scores for Mis after smoothing on the graph are generally higher than those for Que, Sug, or Com. In other words, the graph-based method is highly sensitive to class differences when multi-class prediction is converted from single-class predictions on a scheme like one-vs-all.

In contrast, transductive SVM does not suffer much from class differences according to Figure 7, proving to be more suitable for multi-class classification than graph-based label propagation.

5.3 Summary

For the task of recognizing speech acts in Twitter, we have made some interesting findings from the extensive empirical study. To wrap up, let's summarize the most important of them in the following.

1) Semi-supervised learning approaches, especially transductive SVM, perform comparably to supervised learning approaches, such as inductive SVM, with considerably less training data and lower training/test ratio. Increasing training data cannot improve performance proportionately.

2) Transductive SVM proves to be more effective than graph-based label propagation for our task. The performance of the latter is hurt by two factors: a) the inappropriate assumption about similar tweets having the same speech act and b) its vulnerability to class differences under the one-vs-all multi-class conversion scheme.

3) For supervised learning as well as semi-supervised learning for multi-class classification, training data imbalance poses no lesser threat than training data deficiency.

6. Conclusion and Future Work

Speech act recognition in Twitter facilitates content-based user behavior study. Realizing that it is obsessed with insufficient training data, we start where previous research left.

We are not aware of previous study of semi-supervised learning of speech acts in Twitter and in this paper we contribute to scalable speech act recognition by drawing conclusions from extensive experiments. Specifically, we

1) extend the work of (Zhang et al. 2011) by establishing the practicality of semi-supervised learning that leverages the knowledge of unlabeled data as a promising solution to insufficient training data;

2) show that transductive SVM is more effective than graph-based label propagation for our problem, which aptly extends the maximal margin approach to unlabeled data and is more amenable to the multi-class scenario;

3) provide detailed empirical evidences of multi-class and single-class results, which can inform future extensions in this direction and design of practical systems.

At this stage, we are not sure whether the one-vs-all scheme is a bottleneck to one class-oriented classifiers (it appears to be so for the graph-based method). Therefore we will next explore other multi-class conversion schemes and also consider semi-supervised learning using inherently multi-class classifiers such as Naïve Bayes or Decision Tree. In the future, we will also explore unsupervised approaches to recognizing speech acts in Twitter.

Acknowledgments

The work described in this paper was supported by the grants GRF PolyU 5217/07E and PolyU 5230/08E.

References

Austin, J. 1962. *How to Do Things with Words*. Oxford: Oxford University Press.

Cohen, W., Carvalho, V., and Mitchell, T. 2004. Learning to Classify Email into "Speech Acts". In *Proceedings of Empirical Methods in Natural Language Processing (EMNLP-04)*, 309–316.

Crystal, D. 2006. *Language and the Internet, 2nd edition*. Cambridge, UK: Cambridge University Press.

Crystal, D. 2011. *Internet linguistics*. London: Routledge.

Culp M. and Michailidis, G. 2007. An Iterative Algorithm for Extending Learners to a Semisupervised Setting. In *The 2007 Joint Statistical Meetings (JSM)*.

Deshpande S. S., Palshikar, G. K., and Athiappan, G. 2010. An Unsupervised Approach to Sentence Classification, In *International Conference on Management of Data (COMAD 2010)*, Nagpur, India.

Dhillon, R., Bhagat, S., Carvey, H., and Shriberg, E. 2004. *Meeting Recorder Project: Dialog Act Labeling Guide*. Technical report, International Computer Science Institute.

Erkan, G., Özgür, A., and Radev, D. 2007. Semi-Supervised Classification for Extracting Protein Interaction Sentences Using Dependency Parsing. In *Proceedings of the 2007 Joint Conference on Empirical Methods in Natural Language Processing and Computational Natural Language Learning*, 228–237.

Feng, D., Shaw, E., Kim, J., and Hovy. E. H. 2006. Learning to Detect Conversation Focus of Threaded Discussions. In *Proceedings of HLT-NAACL*, 208–215.

Haffari G.R. and Sarkar. A. 2007. Analysis of semi-supervised learning with the Yarowsky algorithm. In *23rd Conference on Uncertainty in Artificial Intelligence (UAI)*.

Jeong, M., Lin, C-Y., and Lee, G. 2009. Semi-supervised Speech Act Recognition in Emails and Forums. In *Proceedings of EMNLP*, pages 1250–1259.

Joachims, T. 1999. Transductive Inference for Text Classification using Support Vector Machines. In *Proceedings of the 16th International Conference on Machine Learning (ICML)*.

Jurafsky, D., Shriberg, E., and Biasca, D. 1997. *Switchboard SWBD-DAMSL Labeling Project Coder's Manual, Draft 13*. Technical report, University of Colorado Institute of Cognitive Science.

Medlock, B., and Briscoe, T. 2007. Weakly Supervised Learning for Hedge Classification in Scientific Literature. In *Proceedings of the 45th Annual Meeting of the Association of Computational Linguistics*, 992–999.

Searle, J. 1975. Indirect speech acts. In P. Cole and J. Morgan (eds.), *Syntax and semantics, vol. iii: Speech acts* (pp. 59–82). New York: Academic Press.

Stolcke, A., Ries, K., Coccaro, N., Shriberg, E., Bates, R., Jurafsky, D., Taylor, P., Martin, R. Van Ess-Dykema, C., and Meteer, M. 2000. Dialogue Act Modeling for Automatic Tagging and Recognition of Conversational Speech. *Computational Linguistics*, 26(3):339–373.

Vapnik, V. 1998. *Statistical Learning Theory*. New York: John Wiley & Sons.

Yarowsky, D. 1995. Unsupervised Word Sense Disambiguation Rivaling Supervised Methods. In *Proceedings of the 33rd Annual Meeting of the Association for Computational Linguistics (ACL-1995)*, 189–196.

Zhang, R., Gao, D., and Li, W. 2011. What Are Tweeters Doing: Recognizing Speech Acts in Twitter. In *AAAI-11 Workshop on Analyzing Microtext*.

Zhou, D., Bousquet, O., Lal, T. N., Weston, J., and Scholkopf, B. 2004. Learning with Local and Global Consistency. *Advances in Neural Information Processing Systems (NIPS), vol. 16*, Cambridge, MA: MIT Press.

Zhu, X., Ghahramani, Z., and Lafferty, J. D. 2003. Semi-supervised Learning Using Gaussian Fields and Harmonic Functions. In *Proceedings of the Twentieth International Conference on Machine Learning (ICML)*, 912–919, Washington, DC.

Zhu, X. and Goldberg, A. B., 2009. *Introduction to Semi-Supervised Learning*. Morgan & Claypool Publishers.

Topic Classification of Blog Posts Using Distant Supervision

Stephanie D. Husby
University of Alberta
shusby@ualberta.ca

Denilson Barbosa
University of Alberta
denilson@ualberta.ca

Abstract

Classifying blog posts by topics is useful for applications such as search and marketing. However, topic classification is time consuming and error prone, especially in an open domain such as the blogosphere. The state-of-the-art relies on supervised methods, requiring considerable training effort, that use the whole corpus vocabulary as features, demanding considerable memory to process. We show an effective alternative whereby *distant* supervision is used to obtain training data: we use Wikipedia articles labelled with Freebase *domains*. We address the memory requirements by using only named entities as features. We test our classifier on a sample of blog posts, and report up to 0.69 accuracy for multi-class labelling and 0.9 for binary classification.

1 Introduction

With the ever increasing popularity of blogging grows the need of finding ways for better organizing the *blogosphere*. Besides identifying SPAM from legitimate blogs, one promising idea is to *classify* blog posts into *topics* such as travel, sports, religion, and so on, which could lead to better ways of exploring the blogosphere. Besides navigation, blog classification can be useful as a data preprocessing step before other forms of analysis can be done: for example companies can view the perception and reception of products, movies, books and more based on opinions in blogs of different segments.

We approach the problem by using machine learning. In particular, in the development of a learning-based classifier, two crucial tasks are the choice of the features and the building of training data. We adopt a novel approach when selecting features: we use an off-the-shelf Named Entity Recognition (NER) tool to identify entities in the text. Our hypothesis is that one can detect the topic of a post by focusing on the entities discussed in the post. Previous text classification tools use the entire vocabulary as potential features, which is a superset of our feature set. Our results show that despite using a smaller feature set, our method can achieve very high accuracy.

Obtaining training data is a challenge for most learning tools, as it often involves manual inspection of hundreds or thousands of examples. We address this by using *distant supervision*, where a separate dataset is used to obtain training data for the classifier. The distant dataset used here is Freebase[1], which is an open online database, along with related Wikipedia articles. The classes in our tests are *domains* in Freebase, which are defined by their curators.

Summary of Results. For our evaluation, we use a large sample of blog posts from a public snapshot of the blogosphere, collected around 2008. These posts are manually labeled by volunteers (undergraduate students in Computing Science), and used as the ground-truth test data.

Our results indicate that training a classifier relying on named entities using Freebase and Wikipedia, can achieve high accuracy levels on manually annotated data. We also identify some potential problems related to selecting the categories to be used in the classification. Overall, our results indicate that robust classifiers are possible using off-the-shelf tools and freely available

[1] http://www.freebase.com/.

Proceedings of the 13th Conference of the European Chapter of the Association for Computational Linguistics, pages 28–36, Avignon, France, April 23 - 27 2012. ©2012 Association for Computational Linguistics

training data.

2 Related Work

Our work is related to topic identification techniques such as Latent Dirichlet Analysis (LDA), Latent Semantic Analysis (LSA) and Latent Semantic Indexing (LSI) (Steyvers and Griffiths, 2007). These techniques infer possible topic classes, and use unsupervised learning (clustering) approaches. In contrast, our technique allows the specification of classes (topics) *of interest* and attempts to classify text within those classes only. Next we discuss two other lines of work more closely related to ours.

Blog classification. There have been few attempts at classifying blog posts by topic. Most previous methods focus on classification of the authors and the sentiment of the posts.

Ikeda *et al.* (2008) discussed the classification of blog authors by gender and age. They use a semi-supervised technique and look at the blogs in groups of two or more. These groupings are based on which are relatively similar and relatively different. They assume that multiple entries from the same author are more similar to each other than to posts from other blogs, and use this to train the classifier. The classifier they use is support vector machines, and the bag-of-words feature representation. Thus, they consider all unique words in their classification. They find their methods to be 70-95% accurate on age classification, depending on the particular age class (*i.e.* the 20s vs the 30s class is more difficult to distinguish than the 20s vs the 50s) and up to 91% accurate on gender identification. This is quite different than the approach presented here, as we are examining topic classification.

Yang *et al.* (2007) consider the sentiment (positive or negative) analysis of blog posts. Their classifier is trained at the sentence level and applied to the entire document. They use emoticons to first create training data and then use support vector machines and conditional random fields in the actual classification. They use individual words as features and find that conditional random fields outperform support vector machines. This paper works both with blog posts and distance learning based on the emoticons, however this type of distant supervision is slightly different than our approach. It may also be referred to as using weakly labeled data.

Elgersma and de Rijke (2008) classify blogs as personal vs non-personal. The authors define personal blogs as diary or journal, presenting personal accounts of daily life and intimate thoughts and feelings. They use the frequency of words more often used in personal blogs versus those more frequently used in general blogs, pronouns, in-links, out-links and hosts as the features for the blogs. They then perform supervised training on the data using a set of 152 manually labeled blogs to train their classifier. The results show that the decision tree method produced the highest accuracy at about 90% (Elgersma and de Rijke, 2008).

A work which looks at true topic classification of blogs, as is being done here, is that of Hashimoto and Kurohashi (2008), who use a *domain dictionary* to classify blog posts without machine learning (i.e., using a rule-based system). They use keywords for each domain, or category as the basis for classification. They then create a score of a blog post based on the number of keywords from each domain; the domain with the highest count becomes the category for that post. They also expand the keywords in their domain by adding new words on the fly. This is done by taking an unknown word (one that does not currently exist in a domain) and attempting to categorize it using its online search results and/or Wikipedia article. They attempt to classify the results or article and then, in turn, classify the word. They find their classification method to be up to 99% accurate. This idea can be related to the use of Freebase as the domain dictionary in the current problem, but will be expanded to include machine learning techniques, which these authors avoid.

Distant supervision. Distant supervision is a relatively new idea in the field of machine learning. The term was first introduced by Mintz *et al.* (2009) in 2009 in their paper on *relation extraction*. The idea is to use facts in Freebase to obtain training data (i.e., provide distant supervision), based on the premise that if a pair of entities that have a relation in Freebase, it will likely be expressed in some way in a new context. They found their approach to be about 66-69% accurate on large amounts of data. Although the goal of their work (namely, extracting relations from the text) was different from ours, the use of Freebase and entities is directly related to the work presented here.

Go *et al.* (Go et al., 2009) use distant supervision to label the sentiment associated with Twitter posts. They use tweets containing emoticons to label the training data, as follows. If a tweet contains a :) or an : (then it is considered to have a positive or a negative sentiment. Those tweets with multiple emoticons were discarded. Then emoticons themselves are *removed* from all data (to avoid them being used as features), and the labeled data is used to train the classifier. They found their approach to be around 78-83% accurate using several different machine learning techniques (Go et al., 2009). The authors do not discuss their feature representations in detail, but make use of both unigrams and bigrams.

Phan *et al.* (Phan et al., 2008) consider using a *universal data set* to train a classifier for web data similar to blogs . This idea is very similar to the concept of distant supervision. They consider Wikipedia and MEDLINE, as universal data sets, and they use the maximum entropy as their classifier. They apply their methods to two problems, topic clustering of web search results and disease classification for medical abstracts; they report accuracy levels around 80%.

3 Method

Our hypothesis is that one can predict the topic of a blog post based on "what" that post is about. More precisely, we focus on the recognizable named entities that appear in the blog post. Our intuition is that if a blog post mentions "Barack Obama" and the "White House" prominently, it is probably a post about politics. On the other hand, a post mentioning "Edmonton Oilers" and "Boston Bruins" is most likely about hockey. Naturally, there will be posts mentioning entities from different topics, say for example, a comment about the president attending a hockey game. In such cases, our hypothesis is that the other entities in the same post would help break the tie as to which class the post belongs to.

Our method consists of using a classifier trained with all topics of interest. We obtain training data using distant supervision, as follows. The topics come from Freebase, an open, online database compiled by volunteers. At the time of writing, it contains approximately 22 million objects which belong to one or more of a total of 86 domains. Each object in Freebase is a unique person, place, thing or concept that exists in the world. An example of an entity would be "Barack Obama" or "republican". A major data source for Freebase is Wikipedia; indeed, there is even a one-to-one mapping between articles in Wikipedia and the corresponding objects in Freebase.

Category	Articles	Distinct Entities
government	2,000	265,974
celebrities	1,605	85,491
food & drink	2,000	70,000
religion	2,000	175,948
sports	2,000	189,748
travel	2,000	125,802
other	2,000	384,139

Table 1: Topic categories chosen from Freebase domains

Discussion. Our motivation to use Freebase and Wikipedia comes from their large size and free availability, besides the fact these are fairly high quality resources–given the dedication of their contributors. It should be noted that this is a perfect example where distant supervision comes as an ideal approach, in the sense that the classification of objects into domains (i.e., topics) is done manually, and with great care, leading to high quality training data. Moreover, the nature of both datasets, which allow any web user to update and contribute to them, leads us to believe they will remain up-to-date, and will likely contain mentions to recent events which the bloggers would be discussing. Thus, one should expect a high overlap between the named entities in these resources and the blog posts.

3.1 Classifying Blog Posts

The classification of blog posts by topic is done by using the named entity recognition tool to extract all named entities (features) for the blog post, and feeding those to the topic classifier. We consider two classification tasks:

- **Multi-class**: In this case, we are given a blog post and the task is to determine which of the 7 topics (as in Table 1) it belongs to.

- **Binary classification:** In this case, we are given a blog post and a specific topic (i.e.,

	Blog (Test) Data		Wikipedia (Training) Data	
	words/post	**entities/post**	**words/article**	**entities/article**
celebrities	420	49	2,411	311
food & drink	256	28	1,782	144
government	20,176	2,363	6,013	803
other	395	50	10,930	1,245
religion	516	52	3,496	402
sports	498	73	4,716	741
travel	359	41	2,101	239

Table 2: Average word count and entity count per blog post and per Wikipedia article.

class), and the task is to determine whether or not the post belongs in that topic.

The multi-class task is more relevant in an exploratory scenario, where the user would browse through a collection of posts and use the classifier as a means to organize such exploration. The binary classification, on the other hand, is more relevant in a scenario where the user has a specific need. For example, a journalist interested in politics would rather use a classifier that filtered out posts which are not relevant. By their nature, the binary classification task demands higher accuracy.

Features The only features that make sense to use in our classification are those named entities that appear both in the training data (Wikipedia) and the test data (the blog posts). That is, we use only those entities which exist in at least one blog post **and** in at least one Wikipedia article. It is worth mentioning that this reduces drastically the memory needed for classification, compared to previous methods that use the entire vocabulary as features.

Each data point (blog or Wikipedia article) is represented by a vector, where each column of the vector is an entity. Two feature representations were created:

- **In-out:** in this representation we record the presence (1) or absences (0) of the named entity in the data point; and
- **Count:** in this representation we record the number of times the named entity appears in the data point.

	In-Out		Count	
	10-Fold	*Test*	*10-Fold*	*Test*
NB	0.59	0.37	0.51	0.29
SVM	0.26	0.18	0.49	0.22
NBM	0.71	0.57	0.68	**0.60**

Table 3: Summary of Accuracy on Multi-Class Data

4 Experimental Design

We collected the training data as follows. First, we discarded generic Freebase domains such as *Common* and *Metaweb System Types*, which do not correspond to meaningful topics. We also discarded other domains which were too narrow, comprising only a few objects. We then concentrated on domains for which we could find many objects and for which we could perform a reasonable evaluation. For the purposes of this paper, the 7 domains shown in Table 1 were used as topics. For each topic, we find all Freebase objects and their corresponding Wikipedia articles, and we collect the 2,000 longest articles (as those are most likely to contain the most named entities). The exception was the celebrities topic, for which only 1,605 articles were used. From these articles, we extract the named entities (i.e., the features), thus obtaining our training data. In the end, we used 4,000 articles for each binary classification experiment and 13,605 for the multi-class one.

As for test data, we used the ICWSM 2009 Spinn3r Blog Dataset (Burton et al., 2009), which was collected during the summer of 2008, coinciding with the build-up for the 2008 Presidential Elections in the US. In total, the collections has approximately 25M blog posts in English. For

a	*b*	*c*	*d*	*e*	*f*	*g*		← *classified as*
0	0	0	0	0	0	50	*a*	*celebrities*
0	0	0	0	0	0	50	*b*	*food & drink*
0	0	15	27	0	0	8	*c*	*government*
0	0	0	0	0	0	50	*d*	*other*
0	0	0	0	0	0	50	*e*	*religion*
0	0	0	0	0	0	50	*f*	*sports*
0	0	0	0	0	0	50	*g*	*travel*

Table 4: Confusion Matrix of SVM on Test Set with In-Out Rep.

our evaluations, we relied on volunteers[2] who labeled hundreds of blogs, chosen among the most popular ones (this information is provided in the dataset), until we collected 50 blogs for each category. For the binary classifications, we used 50 blogs as positive examples and 200 blogs randomly chosen from the other topics as negative examples. For the multi-class experiment, we use the 350 blogs corresponding to the 7 categories.

Both the blogs and the Wikipedia articles were tagged using the Stanford Named Entity Recognizer (Finkel et al., 2005), which labels the entities according to these types: *Time, Location, Organization, Person, Money, Percent, Date,* and *Miscellaneous*. After several tests, we found that *Location, Organization, Person* and *Miscellaneous* were the most useful for topic classification, and we thus ignored the rest for the results presented here. As mentioned above, we use only the named entities in both the training and test data, which, in our experiments, consisted of 14,995 unique entities.

Classifiers. We performed all our tests using the Weka suite (Hall et al., 2009), and we tested the following classifiers. The first was the Naive Bayes (John and Langley, 1995) (NB for short), which has been successfully applied to text classification problems (Manning et al., 2008). It assumes attribute independence, which makes learning simpler when the number of attributes is large. A variation of the NB classifier, called Naive Bayes Multinomial (NBM) (McCallum and Nigam, 1998), was also tested, as it was shown to perform better for text classification tasks in which the vocabulary is large (as in our case). Finally, we also used the LibSVM classifier (Chang and Lin, 2001) (SVM), which is an implementation of support vector machines, a binary linear classifier. The results reported in this paper were obtained with LibSVM's default tuning parameters. SVMs are often used successfully in text classification problems (Ikeda et al., 2008; Yang et al., 2007; Go et al., 2009). These classifiers were chosen specifically due to their success rate with text classification as well as with other applications of distant supervision.

[2] Undergraduate students in our lab.

	In-Out		**Count**	
	10-Fold	*Test*	*10-Fold*	*Test*
NB	0.66	0.59	0.58	0.32
SVM	0.33	0.22	0.53	0.22
NBM	0.76	0.64	0.72	**0.64**

Table 5: Summary of Accuracy on Multi-Class without *Travel*

a	*b*	*c*	*d*	*e*		← *classified as*
46	0	0	3	1	*a*	*celebrities*
3	25	21	0	1	*b*	*government*
40	2	0	3	5	*c*	*other*
5	1	1	43	0	*d*	*religion*
13	0	0	0	37	*e*	*sports*

Table 6: Confusion Matrix of NB on Test Set with In-Out Rep

5 Experimental Results

We now present our experimental results, starting with the multi-class task, in which the goal is to classify each post into one of 7 possible classes (as in Figure 1).

Accuracy in the Multi-class Task We report accuracy numbers both for 10-fold cross validation (on the training data) as well as on the manually labelled blog posts (test data). The summary of results is given in Table 3. Accuracy as high as 60% was obtained using the NBM classifier. The standard NB technique performed quite poorly in this case; as expected, NBM outperformed NB by a factor of almost two, using the count representation. Overall, the count representation produced better results than in-out on the test data, while losing on the cross-validation tests. Surprisingly, SVM performed very poorly in our tests.

These results were not as high as expected, so

	In-Out		Count	
	10-Fold	*Test*	*10-Fold*	*Test*
NB	0.70	0.60	0.62	0.40
SVM	0.47	0.38	0.67	0.40
NBM	0.79	0.67	0.76	**0.69**

Table 7: Summary of Accuracy on Multi-Class sans Travel, Food

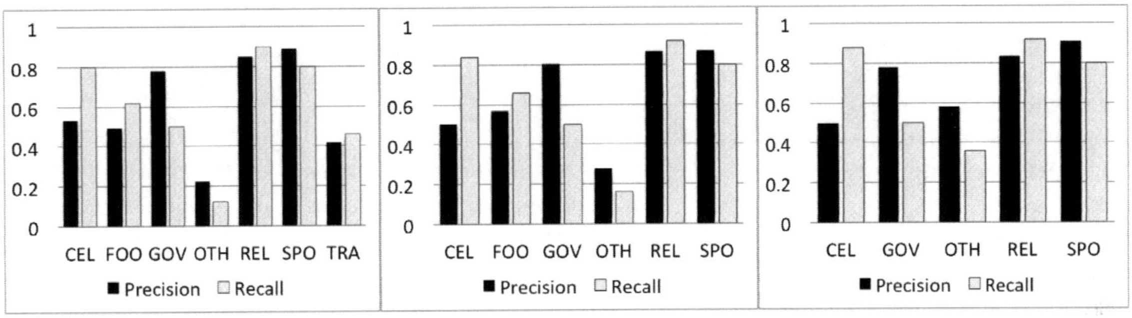

Figure 1: Precision and Recall for Multi-Class Results Using Count Representation. Legend: CEL (Celebrities), FOO (food & drink), GOV (government), OTH (other), REL (religion), SPO (sport), TRA (travel).

we inspected why that was the case. What we found was that the classifiers were strongly biased towards the travel topic: NB, for instance, classified 211/350=60% of the samples that way, instead of the expected 14% (50/350). In the case of SVM, this effect was more pronounced: 88% of the posts were classified as *travel*. Table 4 shows the confusion matrix for the worst results in our tests (SVM with in-out feature representation), and fully illustrates the point.

We then repeated the tests after removing the *travel* topic, resulting in an increase in accuracy of about 5%, as shown in Table 5. However, another inspection at the confusion matrices in this case revealed that the *food & drink* class received a disproportionate number of classifications.

The highest accuracy numbers we obtained for the multi-class setting were when we further removed the *food & drink* class (Table 7). Consistent with previous results, our highest accuracy was achieved with NBM using the count feature representation: 69%. Table 6. gives the confusion matrix for this task, using NB. We can see that the posts are much better distributed now than in the previous cases, approximating the ideal confusion matrix which would have only non-zero entries in the diagonal, signifying all instances were correctly classified.

Recall in Multi-Class experiment. Accuracy (or precision, as used in information retrieval) measures the fraction of correct answers among those provided by the classifier. A complementary performance metric is recall, which indicates the fraction of correctly classified instances out of the total instances of the class. Figure 1 shows the breakdown of precision and recall for each class using the NBM classifier, using the Count feature representation for the tests with all 7 classes (a), as well as after removing *travel* (b) and both *travel* and *food&drink* (c).

As one can see, the overall accuracy by class does change (and improves) as we remove *travel* and then *food&drink*. However, the most significant change is for the class *other*. On the other hand, both the accuracy and recall for *celebrities*, *religion* and *sports* remain virtually unchanged with the removal of these classes.

Discussion of Multi-class results. One clear conclusion from our tests is the superiority of NBM using Count features for this task. The margin of this superiority comes somewhat as a surprise in some cases, especially when one compares against **SVM**, but does not leave much room for argument.

As expected, some classes are much easier to handle than others. Classes such as *celebrities* are expected to be hard as documents in this topic deal with everything about the celebrities, including their preferences in politics, sports, the food they like and the places they travel. Looking at Figure 1, one possible factor for the relatively lower performance for *travel* and *food & drink* could be that the training data in these categories have the lowest average word count and entity count (recall Table 2). Another category with relatively less counts is *celebrities*, which can also be explained by the lower document count (1,605 available articles relating to this topic in Freebase).

Another plausible explanation is that articles in some classes can often be classified in either topic. Articles in the *travel* topic can include information about many things that can be done and seen around the world, such as the culinary traits of the places being discussed and the celebrities that visited them, or the religious figures that represent them. Thus, one would expect some overlap among the named entities relating to these less well-defined classes. These concepts tie easily into the various other topic categories we have considered and help to explain why misclassification was higher for these cases.

We also observed that with the NBM results, in all three variations of the multi-class experiments, there was a fairly consistent trade-off between recall and precision for the *celebrities* class. The erroneous classification of posts into celebrities could be explained in a similar way to those in *food&travel*. The fact that celebrities can exist in sports, politics, and religion means that many of the posts may fit into two or more classes and explains the errors. The best way to explore this further would be to do multiple class labels per post rather than just choosing a single label.

One interesting point that Figure 1 supports is the following. Recall that the need for the class *other* is mostly to test whether the classifier can handle "noise" (blogs which are too general to be classified). With this in mind, the trend in Figure 1 (increasing classification performance as classes are removed) is encouraging, as it indicates that more focused classes (e.g., *religion* and *sports*) can actually be separated well by a classifier using distant supervision, even in the presence of less well-defined classes. Indeed, taken to the extreme, this argument would suggest that the performance in the binary classification scenario for such classes would be the highest (which is indeed the case as we discuss next).

5.1 Binary Classification

We now consider a different scenario, in which the task is to perform a *binary* classification. The goal is to identify posts of a specific class amongst posts of all other classes. The percentage of correctly classified posts (i.e. test data) in this task, based on each feature representation can be seen in Table 8.

Overall, all classifiers performed much better in this setting, although NBM still produced consistently better results, with accuracy in the mid-90% level for the count feature representation. It is worth noting that **SVM** performed much better for binary classifications compared to the multi-class experiments, in some cases tying or ever so slightly surpassing other methods.

Also, note that the classifiers do a much better job on the more focused classes (e.g., *religion*, *sports*), just as was the case with the multi-class scenario. In fact, the accuracy for such classes is near-perfect (92% for *religion* and 93% for *sports*).

6 Conclusion

This paper makes two observations. First, our novel approach of using a standard named entity tagger to extract features for classification does not compromise classification accuracy. Reducing the feature contributes to increasing the scalability of topic classification, compared to the state of the art which is to process the entire vocabulary. The second observation is that distant supervision is effective in obtaining training data: By using Freebase and Wikipedia to obtain training data for standard machine learning classifiers, accuracy as high as mid-90% were achieved on our binary classification task, and around 70% for the multi-class task.

Our tests confirmed the superiority of NBM for text classification tasks, which had been observed before. Moreover, our test also showed that this superior performance is very robust across a variety of settings. Our results also show that it is important to consider topics carefully, as there can be considerable overlap in many general classes

	In-Out			Count		
Class	**NB**	**NBM**	**SVM**	**NB**	**NBM**	**SVM**
religion	0.63	0.90	0.80	0.43	0.92	0.81
government	0.96	0.85	0.80	0.88	0.82	0.87
sports	0.62	0.79	0.79	0.90	0.93	0.79
celebrities	0.60	0.68	0.80	0.40	0.76	0.80
average	0.71	**0.81**	0.79	0.65	**0.86**	0.82

Table 8: Accuracy of Binary Classification.

and this can cause misclassification. Obviously, such overlap is inevitable–and indeed expecting that a single topic can be found for each post can be viewed as a restriction. The most straightforward way to overcome this is by allowing multiple class labels per sample, rather than forcing a single classification.

Given the difficulty of the task, we believe our results are a clear indication that distant supervision is a very promising option for topic classification of social media content.

Future Work. One immediate avenue for future work is understanding whether there are techniques that can separate the classes with high overlap, such as *celebrities*, *food&drinks* and *travel*. However, it is very hard even for humans to separate these classes, so it is not clear what level of accuracy can be achieved. Another option is to examine additional features which could improve the accuracy of the classifier without drastically increasing the costs. Features of the blog posts such as link structure and post length, which we disregarded, may improve classification.

Moreover, one could use unsupervised methods to find relations between the named entities and exploit those, e.g., for bootstrapping. A similar idea would be to exploit dependencies among relational terms involving entities, which could easily be done on blogs and the Wikipedia articles. Topic selection is another area for future work. Our selection of topics was very general and based on Freebase domains, but a more detailed study of how to select more specific topics would be worthwhile. For instance, one might want to further classify *government* into political parties, or issues (e.g., environment, energy, immigration, etc.).

Acknowledgements

This was supported in part by NSERC—Natural Sciences and Engineering Research Council, and the NSERC Business Intelligence Network (project Discerning Intelligence from Text).

References

K. Burton, A. Java, and I. Soboroff. 2009. The ICWSM 2009 Spinn3r Dataset. In *Proceedings of the Third Annual Conference on Weblogs and Social Media (ICWSM 2009)*, San Jose, CA.

Chih-Chung Chang and Chih-Jen Lin, 2001. *LIBSVM: a library for support vector machines.*

E. Elgersma and M. de Rijke. 2008. Personal vs non-personal blogs. *SIGIR*, July.

Jenny Rose Finkel, Trond Grenager, and Christopher Manning. 2005. Incorporating non-local information into information extraction systems by gibbs sampling. *Proceedings of the 43nd Annual Meeting of the Association for Computational Linguistics (ACL 2005)*, pages 363–370.

Evgeniy Gabrilovich and Shaul Markovitch. 2006. Overcoming the brittleness bottleneck using wikipedia: enhancing text categorization with encyclopedic knowledge. In *proceedings of the 21st national conference on Artificial intelligence - Volume 2*, pages 1301–1306. AAAI Press.

A. Go, R. Bhayani, and L. Huang. 2009. Twitter sentiment classification using distant supervision. *Processing*, pages 1–6.

Mark Hall, Eibe Frank, Geoffrey Holmes, Bernhard Pfahringer, Peter Reuteman, and Ian H. Witten. 2009. The weka data mining software: An update. *SIGKDD Explorations*, 11.

C. Hashimoto and S. Kurohashi. 2008. Blog categorization exploiting domain dictionary and dynamically estimated domains of unknown words. *Proceedings of ACL-08, HLT Short Papers (Companion Volume)*, pages 69–72, June.

D. Ikeda, H. Takamura, and M. Okumura. 2008. Semi-supervised learning for blog classification.

Association for the Advancement of Artificial Intelligence.

George H. John and Pat Langley. 1995. Estimating continuous distributions in bayesian classifiers. In *Proceedings of the Eleventh Conference on Uncertainty in Artificial Intelligence*, pages 338–345.

Christopher D. Manning, Prabhakar Raghavan, and Hinrich Schütze. 2008. *Introduction to Information Retrieval.* Cambridge University Press.

A. McCallum and K. Nigam. 1998. A comparison of event models for naive bayes text classification. *In AAAI-98 Workshop on Learning for Text Categorization.*

M. Mintz, S. Bills, R. Snow, and D. Jurafsky. 2009. Distant supervision for relation extraction without labeled data. *ACL-IJCNLP '09: Proceedings of the Joint Conference of the 47th Annual Meeting of the ACL and the 4th International Joint Conference on Natural Language Processing of the AFNLP*, 2:1003–1011.

X. Phan, L. Nguyen, and S. Horiguchi. 2008. Learning to classify short and sparse text & web with hidden topics from large-scale data collections. *International World Wide Web Conference Committee*, April.

M. Steyvers and T. Griffiths, 2007. *Latent Semantic Analysis: A Road to Meaning*, chapter Probabilistic topic models. Laurence Erlbaum.

C. Yang, K. Lin, and H. Chen. 2007. Emotion classification using web blog corpora.

A User and NLP-Assisted Strategic Workflow for a Social Semantic OWL 2-Based Knowledge Platform

Jinan El-Hachem
Engineering & Computer Science Department
Concordia University
Montreal, Quebec, Canada
ji_elhac@encs.concordia.ca

Volker Haarslev
Engineering & Computer Science Department
Concordia University
Montreal, Quebec, Canada
haarslev@cse.concordia.ca

Abstract

Originating from a multidisciplinary research project that gathers, around the Semantic Web standards and principles, Social Networking and Natural Language Processing along with some Bioinformatics notions, this paper sheds the light on some of the most critical aspects of the correspondingly adopted framework and real-time knowledge architecture and modeling platform. It recognizes the considerable profits of an appropriate fusion between the aforementioned disciplines, especially via the proper exploitation of OWL 2 (Web Ontology Language) features and novelties, typically OWL 2 language profiles. Accordingly, it proposes a distinctive workflow with well-defined strategies for an ontology-aware user and NLP-assisted flexible and multidimensional approach for the management of the abundantly available Social data. Application scenarios related to awareness and orientation recommender systems based on biomedical domain ontologies for childhood obesity prevention and surveillance are explored as typical proof of concept application areas.

1 Introduction

In parallel with the Semantic Web's extremely active research community lies a continuous and exceptionally rising propagation of the Social Web. A remarkable advancement can be made if a proper methodology for maximizing the cooperation between the two webs can be set. Such a methodology should highly encourage the first Web to bring in its theories and formalisms to the second, in exchange for some of the latter's popularity and proliferation.

An amplified fusion between the Social and the Semantic Webs is indeed a strongly beneficial achievement to both disciplines. It shall solve the foremost problems undergone by each of them, yielding an outcome that by far surpasses the sum of its individual components by endorsing automation, standardization and interoperability, promoting efficient information extraction, querying and aggregations, and providing valuable large data sets to feed the Semantic Web applications from the abundant social networking Web 2.0 sites (SNS). These sites will successively benefit from Semantic Web applications to generate semantically-rich data, and an overall reflection of the henceforth strongly formalized Social Web's network effect on the Semantic Web, boosting its formerly limited usage (Breslin et al., 2009).

By delving into the Semantic Web's main achievements for Social Networking (SN), this research notices a lack in those involving the Semantic Web's advanced findings and relatively complicated vocabularies and grammars, particularly in the endeavors related to OWL 2 (Web Ontology Language) novelties. In addition, it recognizes the major limitations and concerns related to complexity and accuracy when dealing

Proceedings of the 13th Conference of the European Chapter of the Association for Computational Linguistics, pages 37–45,
Avignon, France, April 23 - 27 2012. ©2012 Association for Computational Linguistics

with ontology-aware Natural Language Processing for large amounts of data.

As a consequence, it proposes a promising flexible and multidimensional user and NLP-assisted workflow for social data management encompassing different strategies varying according to prerequisite constraints and concerns. The proposed workflow is highlighted as part of a knowledge architecture and modeling platform that in addition to its possible incorporation of previous efforts, includes formal methods and models for more advanced Semantic Web accomplishments in support of SN.

The paper thus introduces a backbone knowledge base repository while laying a particular emphasis on an anticipated "meta-semantics" model, revealing the numerous advantages it offers such as its particular language and fragment projection capabilities and the considerably gained flexibility whilst addressing a favorable application area along with appropriate corresponding profile reasoning facilities.

Furthermore, the suggested innovative policy for applying ontology-aware pattern-matching grammars for natural language processing, recommends a layered approach that considers preconditioned concerns and constraints to loosen or restrict text parsing procedures. On the other hand, it confers a Web 2.0 user collaboration novelty residing in promoting SN users "rule tagging" assignments that are initiated on account of domain-specific semantic arrangements in the knowledge base repository. This optional user intervention feature determines the semi-automatic as opposed to the fully automatic adopted strategy.

The overall initiative leads to valuable and fruitful foundations of semantically engineered social data for efficient decision support and recommender systems.

Conversely, data and methodologies for relevant application scenarios aiming at awareness and orientation recommender systems based on biomedical domain ontologies are provided to support the different endeavors and provide typical proof of concept application areas.

Following is a summary of the key contributions:

- Highlights on the critical aspects of an inclusive approach and framework for a knowledge architecture and modeling platform, in its comprised layers and methodologies
- A flexible and multi-dimensional social data management strategy
- An analysis of the proposed strategy's sub-approaches encompassing a crucial NLP component
- A description and emphasis on the user's role in assigning "semantic rule tags".

The rest of this paper is organized as follows: in the next section, we provide an overview of some of the related background work. Section 3 presents a very brief overview of the enclosing knowledge framework and platform; in Section 4, the user and NLP-assisted workflow is portrayed and analyzed; Section 5 exposes OWL 2-supported demonstrating scenarios that endow with recommender systems based on an ontology for childhood obesity surveillance. We finally wrap up with a conclusions section that comprises a closing discussion and highlights on future work.

2 Contextual Background Overview

Description Logics (DL) are a family of knowledge representation languages (Baader et al., 2006) having building blocks consisting of three kinds of entities: concepts, roles and individual names. A DL ontology consists of statements called axioms formed based on the different types of entities and separated into three groups: the set of terminological axioms *TBox*, assertional axioms *ABox,* and relational axioms *RBox.*

While the NLP-related background work will be progressively presented in its related Section 4, we will provide herein some general background information related to OWL 2 novelties on the one hand, and to the main relevant Semantic Web realizations for the Social Web on the other.

2.1 OWL 2 and Description Logics Concepts

Relying on Description Logics, OWL 2 was designed to overcome limitations encountered in the initial version of OWL and to compensate for them (W3C, 2009). It presents extended expressivity, convenience features and various capabilities that will prove to be particularly beneficial for the SN typical data expressed in blogs, wikis, feedback updates, etc. OWL 2 profiles are among the novelty aspects that will mostly be referred to across different sections in this paper.

OWL 2 Profiles (also known as tractable fragments are "trimmed-down" versions of OWL 2 DL; they are the result of a simple trade between all-inclusive expressivity and efficient reasoning. Every fragment addresses a favorable application area; it is therefore essential to identify the target scenario in order to apply the accordingly most favorable profile. In terms of reasoning engines, the regular OWL 2 reasoners are applicable; however, more capable specifically designed ones based on every fragment's constructs have been built.

The main profiles presented for OWL 2 are:

- OWL 2 EL: conceived for the reasoning over large-scale ontologies based on the EL++ family of description logics (Baader et al., 2005). This profile offers OWL's expressive features required by large-scale ontologies such as the "Systemised Nomenclature of Medicine - Clinical Terms" (SNOMED-CT) renowned ontology[1].
- OWL 2 QL: enabling conjunctive queries' satisfiability based on the DL-Lite family of description logics (Calvanese et al., 2007), conceived specifically for reasoning with large amounts of data organized consistently with relatively simple schemata.
- OWL 2 RL: a forward-chaining rule processing system supporting conjunctive rules and relying on a rule-based description logics fragment (Grosof et al., 2003) and on parts of OWL Full rule-based implementations (ter Horst, 2005).

2.2 Social Semantic Web Efforts and Ontologies

The main efforts undergone based on a cooperation between the Semantic and the Social Webs have yielded a vast number of interesting SN specifications, ontologies and projects. Some of the main contributions that our framework is set to be compatible with, to reuse and/or extend, are summarized next:

- The Semantically Interlinked Online Community (SIOC[2]) initiative presents an ontology for representing user activities in blogs and forums, thus increasing the integration of the information in online communities. SIOC is a description of online-community information. It offers a means to represent "rich data" from the Social Web in RDF (Bojars et al., 2008).
- The Friend-of-a-Friend (FOAF[3]) is an ontology for describing people along with their relationships. FOAF can be integrated with other Semantic Web vocabularies and has been established as the most broadly used domain ontology on the semantic web (Miller and Brickley, 2010).
- The Meaning of a Tag (MOAT[4]) framework allows the association of tags to semantics, via linking them to knowledge base URIs such as DBpedia (Auer et al., 2007), GeoNames[5], etc. (Passant and Laublet, 2008).

3 Introducing the Overall Framework

The various efforts described in this paper are all enfolded in an already conceptualized framework for a knowledge architecture and modeling platform that we briefly present herein. Figure 1 provides a high level depiction of its main flow, components and layers.

Having as its core aim the extension of the cooperation between the Social and the Semantic Webs via an underlined use of highly developed and expressive Description Logics-based languages - namely OWL 2, this framework comprises: a knowledge base repository to hold the ontological data, rules and axioms, including specialized domain ontologies, and previously defined social semantic ones; a user and natural language processing-assisted approach to parse and detect semantics from SN Website data (to be explored in the next section), as well as dedicated reasoning capabilities to offer a variety of knowledge and information system services and facilities. Typical reasoning services, typically elucidated in (Baader et al., 2006), like classification and subsumption, satisfiability and instance checking, inference discovery and query answering, rule validation and processing, are the means by which the outcome decision support systems capabilities are attainable. The backbone repository (based on the Semantic Meta-Object-Facility, SMOF (OMG, 2010), another OWL 2

[1] www.ihtsdo.org/snomed-ct
[2] www.sioc-project.org
[3] www.foaf-project.org
[4] www. moat-project.org
[5] www.geonames.org

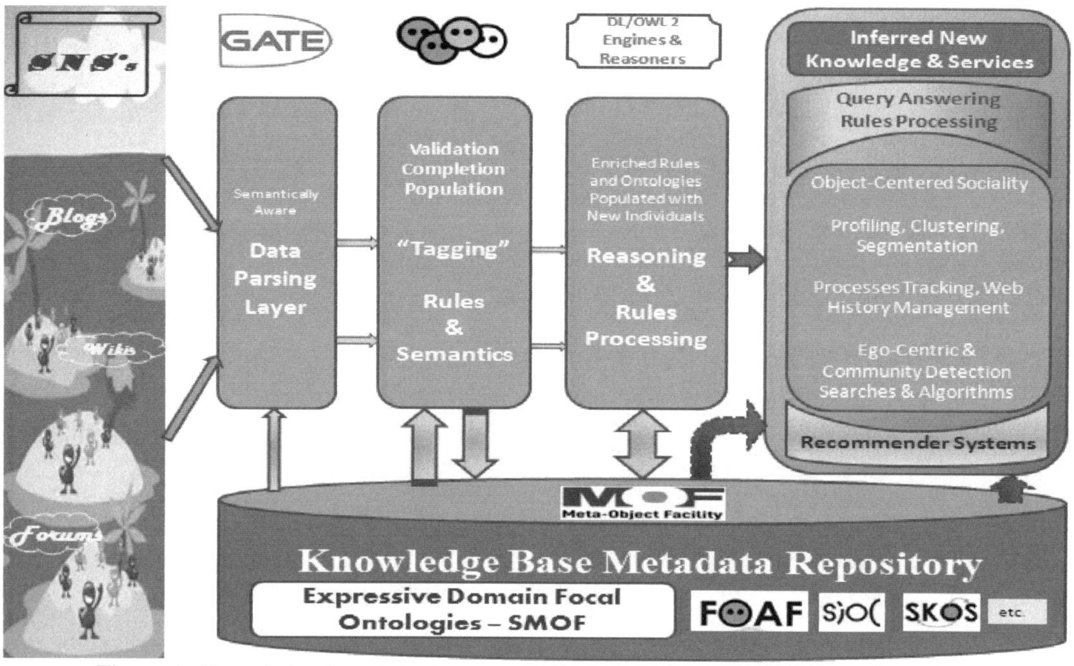

Figure 1- Knowledge-based Architecture and Modeling Platform General Overview

feature) also holds dedicated structures known as meta-semantics structures; they play a crucial role in sorting and grouping the different axioms in the knowledge base, to later allow automatic scaling or downscaling between the OWL 2 sublanguages having varying levels of expressivity. Algorithms and methods that allow this categorization procedure are beyond the scope of this paper, but it is worth noting that this process will have an important impact at the different platforms' levels, notably the NLP-based social data management and ontology population workflow that forms the spotlight of this manuscript.

4 Proposed User and NLP-Assisted Ontology Population Workflow

The proposed strategy that will allow the generation of semantic annotations and the consequent ontological data population is next explored. In a few words, it is a multidimensional and flexible user and NLP-assisted approach relying on SN data constraints and knowledge based prerequisites for automatic or at least semi-automatic domain specific expressive ontology population.

4.1 Online Social Data Sources and NLP Background

The different Web 2.0 platforms such as Twitter[6], Facebook[7], LinkedIn[8], as well as conventional Web logs (blogs), wikis and forums websites all form adequate sources of online SN data to be exploited by our framework, but surely with different levels of availability. Throughout our explored overall framework, we mostly rely on blog and forum posts, due to their accessibility facilities.

The data parsing layer targeting semantic information extraction from the available SN data is based on GATE (the General Architecture for Text Engineering) (Cunningham, 2002). GATE has rapidly grown and evolved to turn into one of the most mature NLP platforms. GATE's effectiveness in ontology-aware language processing has already been demonstrated within several studies and projects, such as KIM[9], a platform for Information Extraction using GATE and targeting large-scale semantic annotation and ontology population based on the PROTON[10] lightweight ontology.

---

[6] www.twitter.com
[7] www.facebook.com
[8] www.linkedin.com
[9] www.ontotext.com/kim
[10] http://proton.semanticweb.org

Some efforts are even directed at more expressive OWL-DL support (Witte et al., 2010). In the scope of our framework, we exploit similar efforts, we further follow our proposed workflow strategy and as a consequence, we reach an automatic or at least semi-automatic creation of the semantic annotations that accordingly lead to the population of our expressive domain ontologies with data compatible with existing relevant SN ontologies (FOAF[11], SIOC[12], etc.).

4.2 User and NLP-Assisted Workflow for Social Data Management

In an ideal situation, a straightforward fully automatic ontology population with instances assigned based on the ontology-aware NLP grammars allows the populated ontology to be readily exploitable by the different OWL reasoners. Constraints and considerations related to the length of the massive social data in question, as well as to the level of expressivity and complexity of the ontology's semantics stimulates the conceptualization and adoption of a more flexible and beneficial strategy and workflow, illustrated in Figure 2, that aims at overcoming or at least limiting the different constraints' significance.

As a particular processing aspect that is proper to our overall previously described framework, a more progressive role held by the SN User is highlighted. A user is accordingly encouraged to explicitly authenticate and even communicate meaningful expressive rules based on provided suggestions. We describe such a role with the terminology of "rules tagging" assignment, enthused by the different SN tagging systems - for instance Flickr[13] and Del.icio.us[14] - that make it possible for users to tag their photos, documents and webpages with simple descriptive taxonomies.

For a more comprehensive interpretation of Figure 2, we start by considering the main constraints to be taken into account a priori, those being the concerns related to the amount of data to be processed, and the complexity of the ontology grammar.

Unless the availability of massive amounts of data to handle is not deemed problematic, predefined mostly impacting subsets of the original data can be arranged in accordance with:

- The blog or forum post title
- The first sentence or paragraph
- The last sentence or paragraph
- A preset number of lines
- A preset number of sentences or paragraphs
- The blogs and forums relevant to a particular SNS that is known to be mostly dedicated to our domain or sub-domain in question
- The blogs and forums satisfying a certain chronological period
- The blogs and forums containing specific keywords (domain critical elements)
- Combinations of the above elements

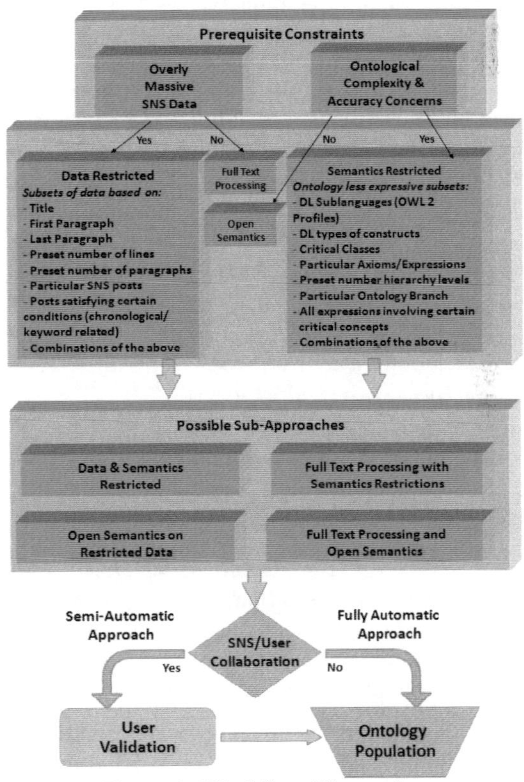

Figure 2: Workflow Illustration

Conversely, unless it is estimated more advantageous to deal with the full ontology, or at least the ensemble of axioms accepted by the employed NLP tool and appropriately developed grammars, semantic strategies can be adopted to deal with expressivity and complex ontology constructs concerns based on:

---

[11] www.foaf-project.org
[12] www.sioc-project.org
[13] www.flickr.com
[14] http://www.delicious.com/

- DL particular less expressive sublanguages, typically the OWL 2 profiles already introduced
- DL specific types of constructs, assessed as mostly critical for the global flow
- Most significant ontology classes or concepts
- Particular key axioms or expressions
- Preset number of levels to go deep in the ontology hierarchy
- A particular branch or set of branches in the ontology hierarchy
- The set of axioms and expressions relevant to certain given concept/s
- Proper combinations of the above

To note that all these conditions and strategies are made possible through the backbone repository's already introduced "meta-semantics" structures.

As a result of all the above, and based on the presented inputs, constraints and limitations, different scenarios can be arranged, and we end up with one of four "possible sub-approaches" as denoted in the illustration:

- Full text processing and open semantics approach, which encompasses thorough analysis and semantic matching covering complicated rules and grammars, which increases implementation complexity, performance and accuracy concerns.
- Open semantics on restricted data approach, in which the originally large amount of data to be processed is minimized.
- Full text processing with semantics restrictions approach, in which we can afford managing large amounts of data, but require a low degree of development complexity, and correspondingly a high accuracy of the attained results.
- Data and semantics restricted approach, which minimizes the large amounts of processable data, as well as performance and accuracy concerns.

These defined NLP-assisted approaches have corresponding meta structures in our metadata repository. Such structures retain information related to the source data's SNS Web 2.0 platforms, to their related conditions and parameters for data and semantics restrictions.

Having reached this stage, the availability or absence of the SNS user collaboration will determine whether the overall strategy towards ontology population is fully or semi automatic. Back to the role of the user in his "rule tagging" assignment, and to lay more emphasis on this role, we highlight the provisional output resulting from the described NLP strategy, which mainly consists of constructed templates of preliminary non-validated sets of semantics, including identity relations and rules, thus made available in a user friendly questionnaire form to optionally confirm, correct or even add more expressive axioms and details. Although not mandatory, this semi-automatic approach that includes a user intervention is deemed extremely advantageous, especially for the open semantics case where the available NLP technology has severe restrictions upon dealing with somewhat complex and expressive vocabularies and ontologies. Nevertheless, it is the overall flexibility provided at both the data and semantics level that will limit the accuracy concerns encountered in traditional NLP approaches.

5 Proof of Concept and Application Scenarios

Our efforts are being carried out under the scope of parents' awareness and orientation. Useful SNS data sources typically beneficial for our domain are "Mom Bloggers". While these sites are extremely active and abundant, most of our data is extracted based on Babycenter[15] (which alone counts more than 20 million users), Canada Moms Blog[16], Raising Children Network[17], among others.

As part of the Brain-to-Society (BtS) (Dubé et al., 2008) research endeavors that call for a whole-of-society (WoS) transformation, centered on the indivudual, the Childhood Obesity [Knowledge] Enterprise (COPE) ontology was conceived (Shaban-Nejad et al., 2011) with the aim of allowing cross-sectional analysis of the obesity domain and consequently generating both generic and customized preventive recommendations. Figure 3 depicts an OntoGraf[18] visualization of a partial view of its major concepts and relationships.

15 www.babycenter.com
16 www.canadamomsblog.com
17 www. raisingchildren.net.au
18 http://protegewiki.stanford.edu/wiki/OntoGraf

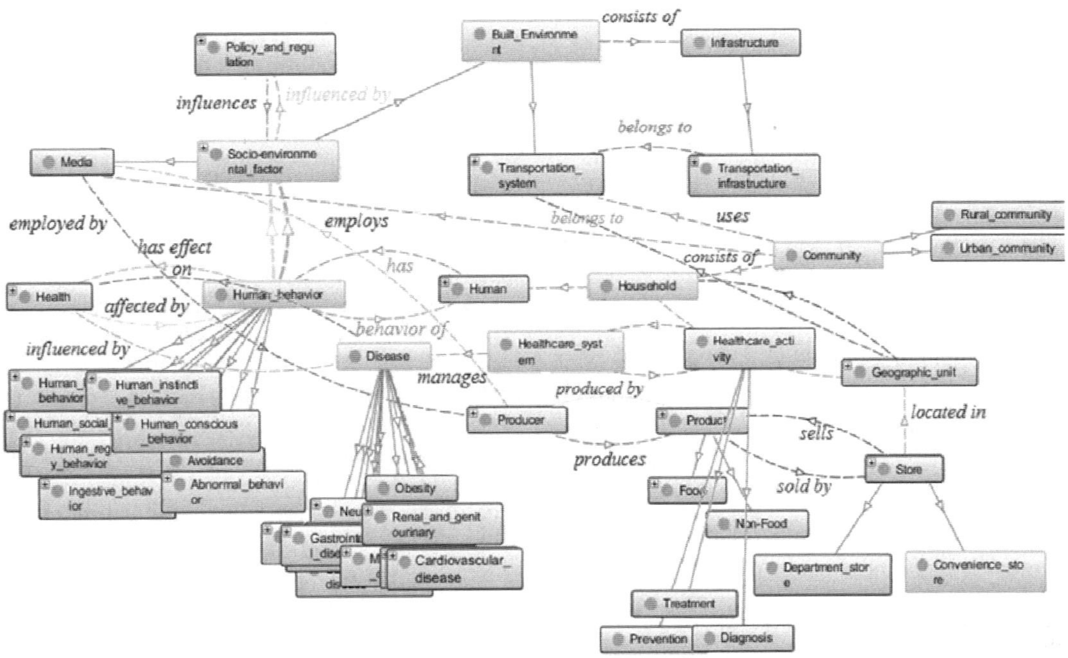

Figure 3 Partial view of the COPE major concepts and their interactions

COPE's data sources (mainly relevant to *TBox* and *RBox* ontological data, apart from the assertional *ABox* data generated from our ontology population workflow) are: RAMQ[19], Canadian Community Health Survey (CCHS[20]) (population health database), CARTaGENE[21], which offer information on medical history, genealogical data, lifestyles, etc..

The COPE ontology was extended and enriched with OWL 2 constructs to maximize its richness and expressivity and be able to take advantage of different language projection and reasoning facilities provided by our real-time knowledge architecture and modeling platform. It has hence served as a source for our semantically aware NLP grammars and Information Extraction algorithms.

To concretize a possible approach from the already proposed strategic workflow (the data and semantics restricted approach), a hybrid methodology that considers the full ontological data related to childhood obesity risks for posts reported in 2012, performs a first phase of processing in which the filtering of all textual data compliant with the specified data restrictions occurs, and then proceeds to the remaining detailed semantics-based analysis.

Table 1 below provides sample generated semantics (represented in DL axioms) along with their contextual natural language interpretation.

DL Axiom	Possible Interpretation
$\exists$*hasRegulatoryDietGoal.Self*	User has a goal/plan to go on a diet
$\exists$*hasDaughter.hasAge(6 m)*	User is a parent of a 6 months-old baby
$\forall$*hasChild.Overweight*	All user's children are overweight
$\exists$*experienceProblem (Fatigue* $\sqcap$ *AbdominalPain)*	Is experiencing health problems consisting in fatigue and abdominal pain
livesIn(MarySt,Grimbsy)	MarySt lives in Grimbsy

Table 1: Illustrated sample semantics with their contextual natural language interpretation

The rest of the flow depends on an optional user validation phase that will precede the population of our knowledge base with the detected ABox assertional data. Interoperability is ensured through an established link between detected individuals and existing FOAF users within the SIOC communities.

Having reached this stage, reasoning procedures can be applied in order to attain the required services for our awareness and orientation recommender systems related to childhood obesity surveillance. Redirection mechanisms, based on the projected languages

[19] Régie de l'assurance maladie du Québec: http://www.ramq.gouv.qc.ca/index_en.shtml

[20] Canadian Community Health Survey (CCHS): http://www.statcan.gc.ca/concepts/health-sante/index-eng.htm

[21] http://www.cartagene.qc.ca/index.php?lang=english

and fragments, target advanced and powerful reasoners and rule engines. For example, Pellet (Sirin et al., 2007) can handle OWL 2 DL and RL, RacerPro (Haarslev and Möller, 2001; Haarslev et al., 2008) can manage a subset OWL 2 DL and OWL 2 EL, HermiT (Motik et al., 2007) and FacT++ (Tsarkov et al., 2006) can cope with OWL 2 DL. On the other hand, the Jena framework (2007) and the database Oracle 11g enable the processing of OWL 2 RL rules, whereas Quill (Thomas and Pan, 2009) a TrOWL (Thomas et al., 2010) component provide OWL 2 QL querying capabilities.

6 Conclusions

Apart from providing a maximal set of consistent and accurate semantics, fostering such a user and NLP-assisted workflow can prove to be advantageous at many levels. We can underline a few extra issues, by considering for example the "Open World Assumption" which is evidently appropriate for the context of textual blog information dealt with in this research: a statement or fact not explicitly mentioned in a blog does not disprove its existence. Nevertheless, to deal with certain critical rules and axioms, for which the availability of accurate data is deemed much more valuable for our working framework, an exclusive approach can be embraced in order to possibly "close the world" related to these critical facts. Closing axioms can be identified in our backbone repository, and presented to the user, inviting them to key in their exact input. Furthermore, the intensional reasoning required in any application involving natural language processing presents DL-safety restrictions, due to conclusions referring to unnamed objects. By offering this user rule tagging facility, we can limit the effects of such constraints. In all cases, relying on a collective effort through which rules and semantics are gathered and validated, before becoming instance and ontology enrichment elements is a much more profitable and effective approach.

A well-populated knowledge base, henceforth enriched with semantically engineered social data, is consequently accessible for further extensive reasoning and analysis. The outcome reached surpasses by far the sum of its social and semantic data components, typically leading to significant services and recommender systems.

Taking into consideration the applicable involved reasoning, the opportunity of identifying, creating and expanding social and semantic networks is presented. Implemented algorithms allow opinion mining, detection of ties and similarities between people, leading to connections via shared interests or any possible common ground areas. For instance, semantic networks are initiated based on the algorithms' ability to retrieve people with same or similar goals, tastes, origins, backgrounds, etc., and to further apply advanced reasoning with the intention of providing suggestions, recommendations, possible solutions, feedbacks, openings, and so on. More straightforward Web Social Networks can be deduced through the users' joint actions and interactions, their created, commented upon, linked to, or similarly annotated contents.

Many aspects of the conclusions and findings will thus be related to the concept of "object-centered sociality", which connects people via the common interests associated with their occupations, hobbies, jobs, etc.

Analogous features accessible through this semantically engineered social data and possibly serving the purposes of recommender systems include the ability to perform:

- User profiling, clustering and segmentation based on certain traits and criteria, all of which are endeavors considered closely related to opinion mining undertakings
- Tracking processes to identify a user's Web history from different Web 2.0 platforms, outlining this user's general overall contributions to the Web and reporting their different activities, goals and problems
- Improved quality of the search process, with ego-centric algorithms and searches to identify a key user's associated or closely related nodes, as well as community detection algorithms to trace two or more key users' surrounding community

In terms of future work, we plan to pursue fostering our different efforts that include implementation and verification tools, looking for the incorporation of maximized sets of rules and Description Logics-based fragments, providing further validating ground for the widest set of the aforementioned potentials and promises.

References

A. Passant, P. Laublet. Meaning Of A Tag: A collaborative approach to bridge the gap between tagging and Linked Data. In Proceedings of the WWW2008 Workshop Linked Data on the Web (LDOW2008), Beijing, China, Apr 2008

A. Shaban-Nejad, D. Buckeridge, D, L. Dubé, COPE: Childhood Obesity Prevention [Knowledge] Enterprise. in Proceedings of AIME 2011, pp. 225-229

B. Grosof, I. Horrocks, R. Volz, S. Decker, Description Logic Programs: Combining Logic Programs with Description Logic, In Proceedings of the 12th Int. World Wide Web Conference (WWW 2003), Budapest, Hungary, 2003

B.Motik, R. Shearer, I. Horrocks, Optimized reasoning in description logics using hypertableaux, in: CADE-07, 2007

D. Calvanese, G.D. Giacomo, D. Lembo, M. Lenzerini, R. Rosati, Tractable reasoning and efficient query answering in description logics: the DL-Lite family, Journal of Automated Reasoning, vol.9, pp. 385-429, 2007

D. Tsarkov, I. Horrocks, FaCT++ description logic reasoner: system description, In Proceedings of the IJCAR 2006, Seattle,WA, USA, 2006

D. Miller, D. Brickley, FOAF Vocabulary Specification, Friend of a Friend Project, http://xmlns.com/foaf/0.1/, 9 August 2010

E. Sirin, B. Parsia, B.C. Grau, A. Kalyanpur, Y. Katz, Pellet: a practical OWL-DL reasoner, Journal of Web Semantics, vol. 5, no. 2, pp. 51-53, 2007

E. Thomas, J. Z. Pan, R-Quill: Reasoning with a Billion Triples, In 8th International Semantic Web Conference (ISWC2009), 2009.

E. Thomas, J. Pan, and Y. Ren, TrOWL: Tractable OWL 2 Reasoning Infrastructure, In Proceedings of the Extended Semantic Web Conference. Springer, 2010

F. Baader, S. Brandt, C. Lutz, Pushing the EL envelope, In Proceedings of the IJCAI 2005, 2005

F. Baader, D. Calvanese, D.L. McGuinness, D. Nardi, P.F. Patel-Schneider, The Description Logic Handbook: Theory, Implementation and Applications, Cambridge University Press, 2006.

H. Cunningham, GATE, a General Architecture for Text Engineering, Journal of Computers and the Humanities, vol. 36, pp. 223-254, 2002

H. J. ter Horst, Completeness, decidability and complexity of entailment for RDF Schema and a semantic extension involving the OWL vocabulary, The Journal of Web Semantics, vol. 3, no.2-3, pp. 79-115, 2005

J.G. Breslin, A. Passant, S. Decker, The Social Semantic Web, Springer, October 2009

Jena - A Semantic Web Framework for Java, URL: http://jena.sourceforge.net, 2007

Object Management Group OMG, MOF Support for Semantic Structures (SMOF) Revised Joint Submission, OMG Document formal/2010-08-06, http://www.omg.org/spec/SMOF/1.0/Source/10-08-06.pdf, 2010

R. Witte, N. Khamis, J. Rilling. Flexible Ontology Population from Text: The OwlExporter, The Seventh International Conference on Language Resources and Evaluation (LREC 2010), pp.3845-3850, May 19-21, 2010, Valletta, Malta.

Systemised Nomenclature of Medicine - Clinical Terms (SNOMED-CT), URL: http://www.ihtsdo.org/snomed-ct/

S. Auer, C. Bizer, G. Kobilarov, J. Lehmann, R. Cyganiak, and Z. Ives, DBpedia: A Nucleus for a Web of Open Data. 6th International Semantic Web Conference, November 2007

The KIM Platform, URL: http://www.ontotext.com/kim/

The PROTON Ontology, URL: http://proton.semanticweb.org

U. Bojars, J.G. Breslin, V. Peristeras, G. Tummarello, S. Decker, Interlinking the Social Web with Semantics, IEEE Intelligent Systems, vol. 23, no. 3, pp. 29-40, 13 May 2008

V. Haarslev, R. Möller, RACER system description, in Proceedings of the IJCAR 2001, Siena, Italy, 2001.

V. Haarslev, R. Möller, and S. Wandelt, The revival of structural subsumption in tableau-based description logic reasoners, In Proceedings of the 2008 International Workshop on Description Logics, 2008.

World Wide Web Consortium W3C, OWL 2 Web Ontology Language Document Overview, http://www.w3.org/TR/owl2-overview/, W3C Recommendation, 27 October 2009

A hybrid framework for scalable Opinion Mining in Social Media: detecting polarities and attitude targets

Carlos Rodríguez-Penagos
Barcelona Media Innovació
Av. Diagonal 177
Barcelona, Spain
carlos.rodriguez @barcelonamedia.org

Jens Grivolla
Barcelona Media Innovació
Av. Diagonal 177
Barcelona, Spain
jens.grivolla @barcelonamedia.org

Joan Codina Fibá
Barcelona Media Innovació
Av. Diagonal 177
Barcelona, Spain
joan.codina @barcelonamedia.org

Abstract

Text mining of massive Social Media postings presents interesting challenges for NLP applications due to sparse interpretation contexts, grammatical and orthographical variability as well as its very fragmentary nature. No single methodological approach can be expected to work across such diverse typologies as twitter micro-blogging, customer reviews, carefully edited blogs, etc. In this paper we present a modular and scalable framework to Social Media Opinion Mining that combines stochastic and symbolic techniques to structure a semantic space to exploit and interpret efficiently. We describe the use of this framework for the discovery and clustering of opinion targets and topics in user-generated comments for the Telecom and Automotive domains.

1 Introduction

Social Media (SM) postings constitute a messy and highly heterogeneous media that nonetheless represent a highly valuable source of information about the attitudes, interests and expectations of citizens and consumers everywhere. This fact has driven a trove of recent research and development efforts aimed at managing and interpreting such information for a wide spectrum of commercial applications, among them: reputation management, branding, marketing design, etc. A diverse array of techniques representing the state of the art run the gamut from knowledge-engineered rule-and lexicon-base approaches that (when carefully crafted) provide high precision in homogeneous contexts, to wide-coverage machine learning approaches that (when suitable development data is available) tackle noisy text with reasonable accuracies in some genres.

As SM channels are as different from each other as, say, spoken text from essay writing, we believe that no single technique, powerful as it may be, is capable of interpreting all domains, genres and channels in the vast universe of SM conversations. Faced with an industrial demand for simultaneous monitoring of heterogeneous opinion sources, our approach has evolved into combining diverse NLP technologies into a robust semantic analysis framework to create a high-granularity representation of user-generated commentaries amenable to machine interpretation.

Analysis of Telecom-related social postings has shown how a modular and scalable analysis framework can combine a veritable arsenal of NLP and data mining techniques into a hybrid application that adapts well to the unique challenges and demands of different Social Media genres.

Section 2 will present the UIMA-Solr framework and components used to process opinionated text, as well as discuss the representational choices made for analysis. Section 3 will frame our approach within the State-of-the-Art of Sentiment analysis and Opinion mining as we interpret it, while Sections 4 and 5 describe data and results of the application of our proposed approach in the context of opinion topic detection and clustering of SM postings in the Telecoms and Automobile domains respectively, and with different textual genres. Finally, Section 6 will focus on the conclusions and future work that presents to us at this point.

Proceedings of the 13th Conference of the European Chapter of the Association for Computational Linguistics, pages 46–52,
Avignon, France, April 23 - 27 2012. ©2012 Association for Computational Linguistics

2 A modular toolset for SM processing

For semantic processing of our data we use a UIMA [1] (Ferrucci & Lally, 2004) architecture plus Solr-based clustering and indexing capabilities. Our choice of UIMA is guided in part by our wish to achieve good scalability and robustness, and that all components can be implemented modularly and in a distributed manner using UIMA-AS (Asynchronous Scale out). Also, UIMA's data representation as CAS objects allows preserving the documents integrity since annotations are added as standoff metadata, without modifying the original information.

Under the UIMA architecture, a hybrid NLP analysis framework is possible, combining powerful Machine Learning modules like Maximum Entropy (ME, OpenNLP) [2] or Conditional Random Fields (CRF, JulieLab), [3] with gazetteer and regular expression matchers and rule-based Noun Phrase chunkers. The basic linguistic processing has a sentence and token identifier, a POS tagger, a lemmatizer, a NP chunker and a dependency parser. In addition, we employ gazetteers to match products, companies, and other entities in text, as well as a hand-crafted lexicon of polar terms created from corpus exploration of Telecom domain text, as well as a regular expression module to detect emoticons when available. Also, two models for Named-Entity recognition were applied using CRF: one trained on conventional ENAMEX Named Entity Recognition and Classification entities, and another trained using data from customer reviews from various domains (Cars, Banking, and Mobile service providers), in order to detect opinion targets and cues. One of the objectives of this relatively straightforward processing (although by no means the only one), was to select candidates for classifiers that could identify both the specific subject of each opinion expressed in text, as well as capture a more general topic of the whole conversation (which conceivably could coincide or not with one of the specific opinion targets). Targets and topics are usually expressed as entity names, concepts or attributes, and thus can appear in language as noun, adjectival, adverbial or even verbal phrases. Opinion cues (or Q-elements) are words, emoticons and phrases that convey the actual attitude of the speaker towards the topics and targets, and a strength and polarity can be attributed to them, both *a priori* and in context.

Our modular processing approach allows customizing the annotation for each domain or genre, since, for example, regular expressions to detect emoticons will be useful for twitter micro-blogging, but less so for more conventional blogs where such sentiment-expression devices are less frequent; Also pre-compiled lists of known entities can provide good target precision while customised distributional models will help discover unlisted names and concepts in text.

The output of the semantic and syntactic processing pipeline is indexed using the Apache Solr framework,[4] which is based on the Lucene engine. This setup allows the implementation of clustering and classification algorithms, allowing us to obtain reliable statistical correlations between documents and entities.

We also developed or adapted a number of visualization components in order to present the data stored in Solr in an interactive page that is conducive to data exploration and discovery by the system's corporate users. At the same time, Carrot2 is connected to Solr and is used to test clustering conditions and algorithms, providing a nice visualization interface. Carrot2 is an open source search results clustering engine (Osiński & Weiss, 2005). It can automatically organize collections of documents into thematic categories.

3 Previous work

Two good overviews of general Opinion Mining and Sentiment Analysis challenges are Pang & Lee (2008) and, focused specifically on customer reviews, Bhuiyan, Xu & Josang (2009). Detecting the subject or targets of opinions is one of the main lines of work within Opinion Mining, and considerable effort has been put into it, since it has been shown to be a highly-domain specific task (consumer reviews will focus on specific products and features, tweets have hashtags to identify topics, blogs can talk almost about anything, etc.).

Outside of user-generated content, Coursey, Mihalcea, & Moen (2009) have suggested using indirect semantic resources, such as the Wikipedia, to identify document topics. For Opinion Mining genres, and extending on Hu & Liu (2004), Popescu & Etzioni (2005) use a combination of Pointwise Mutual Information,

[1] Unstructured Information Management Architecture

[2] http://maxent.sourceforge.net

[3] http://www.julielab.de

[4] http://lucene.apache.org/solr/

relaxation labeling and dependency analysis to extract possible targets and features in product reviews. Kim & Hovy (2006), for example, use thematic roles to establish a relation between candidate opinion holders and opinion topics, while exploiting clustering to improve coverage in their role-labeling. Recent approaches have included adaptation of NER techniques to noisy and irregular text, either by using learning algorithms or by doing text normalization (Locke & Martin, 2009; Ritter, Clark & Etzioni, 2011).

4 Exploring the semantic space of Telecom-related online postings

We collected close to 200,000 postings from various SM sources in a 4 month timeframe, including fairly carefully-written product-oriented forums, blogs, etc., as well as more casually-drafted Facebook and twitter micro-blogging, that discussed Spanish Telecom's services and products. Of these, we randomly sub-selected a representative 190-document sample that was manually marked-up (for a test involving machine learning of cue-polarity-target relationships) by two different human annotators with a 20-document overlap, using simplified annotation guidelines focused on opinion targets, topics, cues and polarities. An interesting observation about the interannotator agreement (but one we can't discuss in detail here) is that with regard to targets one of the human annotators tended more towards complete syntactic units (noun phrases), while the other chose more conceptual and semantic extensions as subjects for the opinions. The 20-document overlap was meant to help us evaluate this guideline development process, but the misalignment of guideline interpretation by the two human annotators made it very difficult to measure any kind of true interannotator agreement. Also, single annotation adjudication was made difficult due to the fact that both interpretations presented valid aspects, and we chose to use each set as an independent evaluation set to detect any unnoticed patterns that could emerge from using one of the other in our training and validation, but those results are inconclusive and merit further research. Since no adjudicator was incorporated in the process to resolve disagreements, the final annotated sets do not constitute a true Gold Standard, but each human-annotated set was used in turn as a benchmark against automatic annotators.

Content elicitation was combined with activity and network mining for an enriched overview of the social conversation ecosystems, but the second aspect won't be discussed here for the sake of brevity. For the same reason, although other aspects of sentiment analysis were performed on this data (cue and polarity detection, for example), we will also restrict the scope of these discussions on the detection and clustering of specific targets and general topics of the opinions expressed in such SM channels. Obviously, a deeper and more textured view of opinionated text is needed to be of any real use, but the overall features, shortcomings and advantages of our chosen approach are adequately discussed even if we restrict this paper to these very specific tasks.

The first series of experiments about clustering using semantics explored the above-mentioned corpus of SM posting that discussed a Spanish Telecom, one of the aims being detecting and aggregating the topics and targets of online opinions. Different processing modules geared towards topic and target detection were compared against each human annotator's choices, but also against each other and to the combined output of each. The main modules involved were: (A) generic NERC, (B) a target and topic NERC model (StatTarg), (C) a Noun Phrase Chunker, and (D) a Gazetteer matcher (Taxonomy). Figures 1 through 4 show, respectively, recall (1) and precision (2) with regard to human annotated topics, and recall (3) and precision (4) with regard to human annotated targets.

The results presented here are the overall performance across genres and domains, since the 190 documents annotated covered the whole range from forums to tweets.

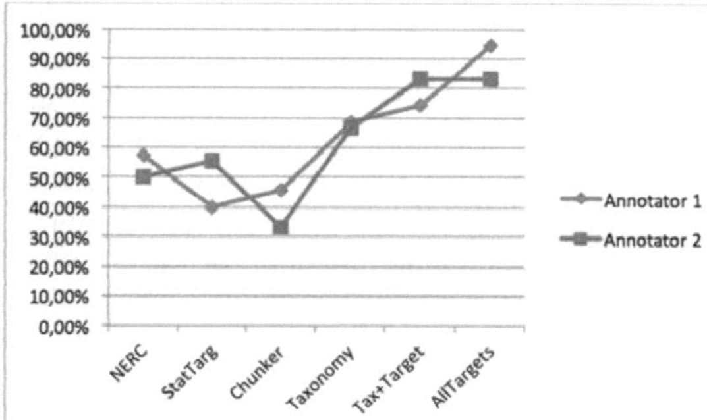

Figure 1. Topic recall

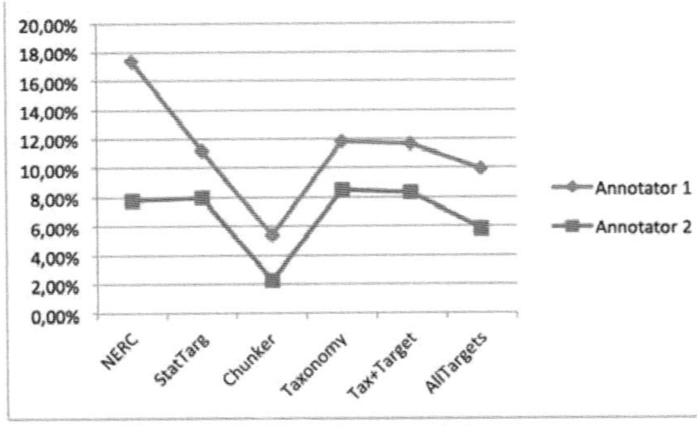

Figure 2. Topic precision

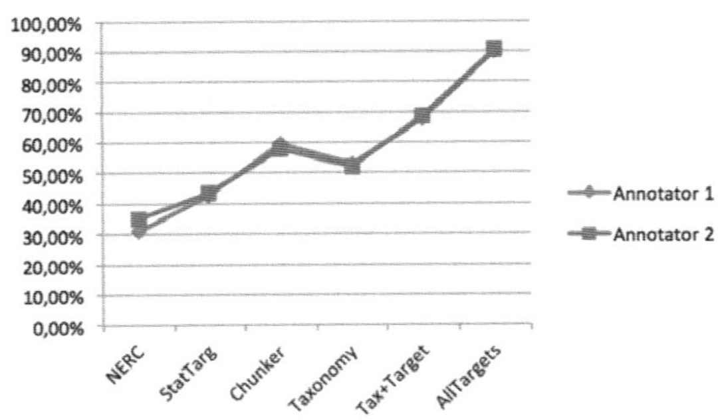

Figure 3. Target recall

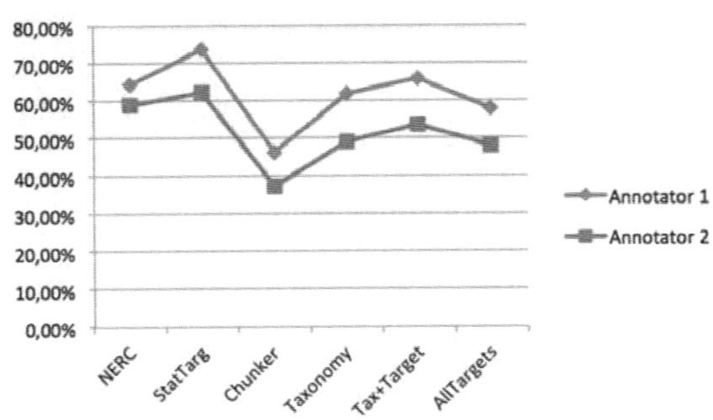

Figure 4. Target precision

For this experiment, and as a guideline for the human annotators, targets were roughly defined as occurrences in the text of objects of opinion, whereas topics where to represent the main focus of the document or message. The annotators usually marked one topic per document, which was almost always also one of the targets.

The customized taxonomy has a good precision with regard to target and topic identification, while the NERC and NP Chunk approaches improve the recall but suffer a bit on precision. Generic NER models have a moderately high precision (63%) with regard to manually annotated targets but rather low recall (specially in genres where capitalization is irregular which hinders NER detection), while NP Chunks present the opposite case: moderately (56%) high recall with low precision. This can be explained in part by the "greediness" of each methodology, with the chunker annotating extensively while the NERC model being much more selective. Another noteworthy result is the strong domain bias of target annotators trained on a Ciao customer reviews for Banking, Automotive and Mobile Service markets. The models implemented through training from multi-domain review sites were found to have medium precision, but very low recall.

The combination of all modules (*AllTargets*, a combination of NERC, Chunker, Taxonomy and StatTarget) had a very high recall of around 90%. With regard to topic detection, the combination of all modules had a recall of 94% and 83%, depending on which gold standard it is compared to (the one created by one expert human annotator or the other), which is an excellent recall level. The precision obtained on topic detection is very low. This, however, is expected as the evaluation is done using all candidates given by the different annotation layers, with no selection process. Since most of the topics are already identified as targets, the key issue here is to identify which of the comment targets is the main topic.

It is important to note that merging the *Chunker* output with that of the rest of the modules improves the recall of the system but the precision becomes low. The main reason is that most targets and topics are noun phrases, but not all noun phrases are targets or topics.

It is important to note that combining the output of different annotation layers (except for the NP chunker) does not reduce overall precision, while greatly increasing recall.

For the clustering experiments, we chose Carrot2's Lingo, a clustering algorithm based on Singular Value Decomposition. We envisioned the content-based clustering as an interactive exploratory tool, rather that providing a single "correct" and definitive set of groupings. Cluster analysis as such is not an automatic task, but an iterative process of knowledge discovery that involves trial and failure. It will often be necessary to modify the preprocessing and adjust parameters until the result achieves the desired properties.

The query "*problem*", for example, sent to some of the telecom forums in May produced groupings suggestive of complaints relating to rates, internet access, SIM chips, SMS, as well as with regard to specific terminal models and companies. Even this limited capability can be helpful for some of our user's market analysis purposes.

The visualization of query-based clustering with detection of target, cues and topics, and the possibility of tracking trends over time, provided a very powerful overview of how consumer attitudes, expectations and complaints about products and services are reflected in dynamic interchanges in various SM channels. These results are available through an online demo[6] (Figure 5, shown for Facebook postings).

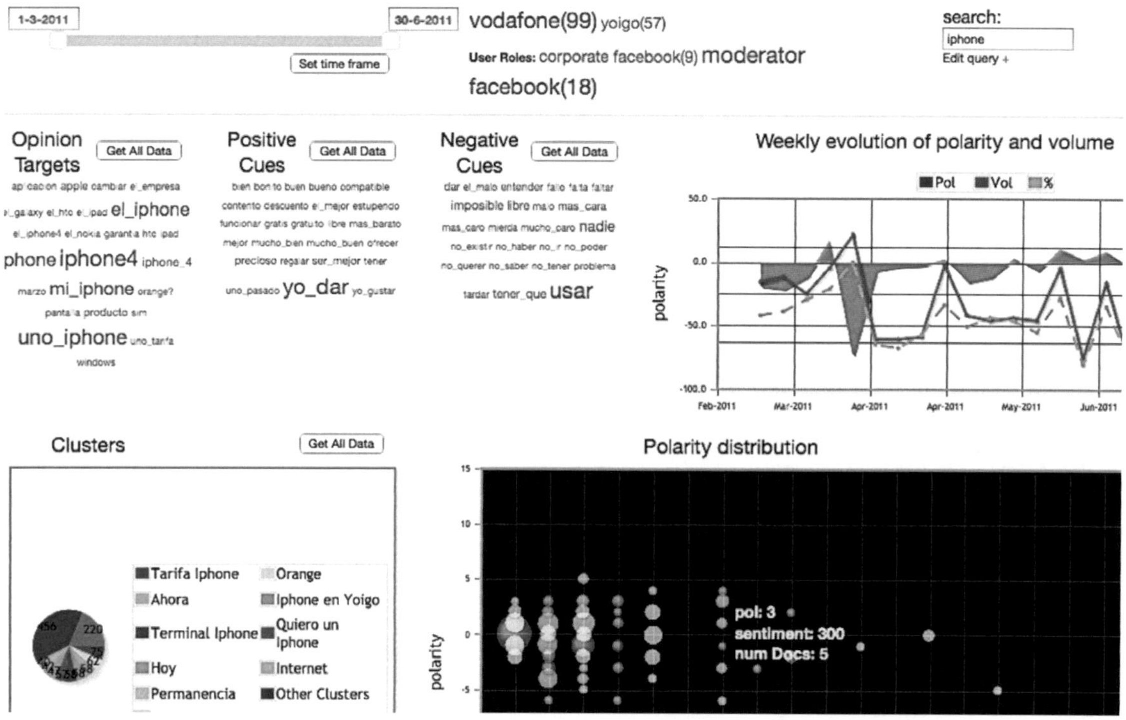

Figure 5. Facebook's "Iphone" semantic exploration (screenshot)

5 Visualizing the evolution of customer opinion

In addition to exploring SM data for the Telecom domain, we performed some experiments using clustering without directly using annotated semantics, but instead using the semantics only for data interpretation. We crawled more than 10,000 customer reviews in the automotive domain in Spanish, along with some metadata that included the numerical ratings added by the reviewers themselves. Using our modular pipeline, we did shallow document clustering followed by linguistic processing that included lemmatization, POS tagging and Named Entity Recognition, in order to allow for analytical exploitation of the community-driven discussion on automobiles, product features and automakers. The most relevant nouns, adjectives, bigrams and named entities from a given query, are projected into a polarity versus time dynamic map. The clustering was performed by the combined use of vector space reduction techniques and the K-means classification paradigm in a completely unsupervised manner. Clusters thus obtained were represented by sets of words that best described them to obtain a view of the emerging terms, trends and features contained in the opinions, with the aim of providing a representation of their collective content. Since evaluating clustering techniques *per se* was not the objective of these experiments, and since a gold standard was not available, the purpose of the system was (A) to validate the coherence of the groupings according to the review's content, and (B) assess if those clusters also aggregate as well along declared global polarity. Although inconclusive from a quantitative point of view, those experiments show the feasibility of leveraging existing Social Media resources in order to develop applications that can visualize and explore the semantic ecosystem of consumer opinions and attitudes, in a cost-effective and efficient manner. A demo of the functionalities of the system described here is also publicly

[6] http://webmining.barcelonamedia.org/Orange/

available.[7]. One cluster, a very positive one (based on the average user rating), is represented by the terms *land-terreno-todoterreno-rover-campo-4x4* (*off-road, field, ground, land, Rover*), while another one, *aceite-garantía-servicio-problemas-años* (*oil-warranty-service-problems-years*), in the lower right side might indicate unhappy reviewers.

6 Conclusion and future work

The results obtained on the Telecom corpus with different automatic annotation layers suggest that a possible improvement in the system could come from researching which combinations of automatic annotators can enhance overall performance, as one module's strength might complement another weaknesses and *vice versa,* so that what one is missing another one can catch. An additional option to increase overall recall is to implement a weighted voting scheme among the modules, allowing calculation of probabilities from the combinations of various annotations that overlap a textual segment.

The fact that combination of annotation layers through simple merging of all annotations has such a great impact on recall while not reducing precision suggests that the different methods are very complementary. We expect to be able to trade off some of the gained recall for much improved precision by applying more sophisticated merging methods.

Another possibility to be explored is using top level dependencies (such as SUBJECT, SENTENCE, etc.) to rank and select the main topic and target candidates using sentence structure configuration. This approach would also ensure that once a polarity-laden cue is identified, the corresponding target could be uniquely identified. This linguistics-heavy approach is feasible only in texts whose characteristics more closely resemble the data used to train the parser.

Our work has helped us focus more clearly many of the challenges faced by any NLP system when used in a new user-generated content: scarce development data, novel pattern and form adaptability, tool robustness, and scalability to massive and noisy text.

One of the lessons learned during these experiences is that keeping a modular hybrid analysis framework can improve matching by either customizing the pipeline to each genre and task requirements, or by combining the results of different approaches to benefit from each one's strengths while minimizing each one's weaknesses. Extracting opinion centered information from highly heterogeneous text and from multitudes of authors will never be as straightforward as, say, doing IE on newswire or financial news, but it should be feasible and useful by using the right toolset. We are in the process of using crowdsourcing to fully annotate vast Spanish and English corpora of opinionated text, which will allow us to perform a better and more fine-grained quantitative analysis of our framework in the near future.

Another lesson learned is that even if high-precision opinion classification is not available (because not enough development data is available, or data is noisy, or for whatever other reason) doing even superficial semantic annotation of the text and unsupervised clustering can help industrial consumer of these technologies understand better what is being said in the Social Media ecosystems. Valuable objectives for a useful opinion mining system do not need to include all possible analyses or state-of-the-art performance.

Going forward, computational exploitation of Social Media and of community-based, data-driven discussions on diverse topics and products is definitely an important facet of future market and business intelligence competencies, since more and more of our activities as citizens, friends and consumers take place in an online environment, where everything seems possible but where also everything we do leaves a trace and has a meaning. Extracting the semantics of collective action enables us to access that meaning.

References

Ritter A, Clark S, Mausam, and Etzioni O (2011). Named Entity Recognition in Tweets: An Experimental Study. Proceedings of the 2011 Conference on Empirical Methods in Natural Language Processing (EMNLP 2011)

Bhuiyan, T., Xu, Y., & Josang, A. (2009). State-of-the-Art Review on Opinion Mining from Online Customers' Feedback. Proceedings of the 9th Asia-Pacific Complex Systems Conference (pp. 385–390).

Coursey, K., Mihalcea, R., & Moen, W. (2009). Using encyclopedic knowledge for automatic topic identification. Proceedings of the Thirteenth Conference on Computational Natural Language Learning, CoNLL '09 (pp. 210–218). Stroudsburg,

[7] http://webmining.barcelonamedia.org/cometa/index_dates

PA, USA: Association for Computational Linguistics.
Ferrucci, D., & Lally, A. (2004). UIMA: an architectural approach to unstructured information processing in the corporate research environment. Natural Language Engineering, 10(3-4), 327–348.
Hu, M., & Liu, B. (2004). Mining and summarizing customer reviews. Proceedings of the tenth ACM SIGKDD international conference on Knowledge discovery and data mining (pp. 168-177). Seattle, WA, USA: ACM. doi:10.1145/1014052.1014073
Kim, S. M., & Hovy, E. (2006). Extracting opinions, opinion holders, and topics expressed in online news media text. Proceedings of the Workshop on Sentiment and Subjectivity in Text (pp. 1–8).
Locke, B., & Martin, J. (2009). Named entity recognition: Adapting to microblogging. University of Colorado.
Osiński and D. Weiss (2005), "Carrot 2: Design of a flexible and efficient web information retrieval framework," Advances in Web Intelligence, pp. 439–444, 2005.
Pang, B., & Lee, L. (2008). Opinion mining and sentiment analysis. Foundations and Trends in Information Retrieval, 2(1-2), 1–135.
Popescu, A. M., & Etzioni, O. (2005). Extracting product features and opinions from reviews. Proceedings of HLT/EMNLP (Vol. 5, pp. 339–346).

Predicting the 2011 Dutch Senate Election Results with Twitter

Erik Tjong Kim Sang and **Johan Bos**
Alfa-informatica
University of Groningen
Groningen, The Netherlands
{e.f.tjong.kim.sang, johan.bos}@rug.nl

Abstract

To what extend can one use Twitter in opinion polls for political elections? Merely counting Twitter messages mentioning political party names is no guarantee for obtaining good election predictions. By improving the quality of the document collection and by performing sentiment analysis, predictions based on entity counts in tweets can be considerably improved, and become nearly as good as traditionally obtained opinion polls.

1 Introduction

Predicting the future is one of human's greatest desires. News companies are well aware of this, and try to predict tomorrow's weather and changes on the stock markets. Another case in point are the opinion polls, of which the news is abundant in the period before political elections. Such polls are traditionally based on asking a (representative) sample of voters what they would vote on the day of election.

The question we are interested in, is whether opinion polls could be conducted on the basis of the information collected by Twitter, a popular microblog website, used by millions to broadcast messages of no more than 140 characters, known as *tweets*. Over the last two years, we have collected a multi-billion-word corpus of Dutch tweets, with the general aim of developing natural language processing tools for automatically analyzing the content of the messages in this new social medium, which comes with its own challenges. When the Dutch Senate elections took place in 2011, we took this as an opportunity to verify the predictive power of tweets.

More concretely, we wanted to test whether by simply counting Twitter messages mentioning political party names we could accurately predict the election outcome. Secondly, we wanted to investigate factors that influence the predictions based on the Dutch tweets.

In this paper we present the results of our experiments. We first summarize related work in Section 2. Then we outline our data collection process (Section 3). The methods we used for predicting election results and the obtained results, are presented in Sections 4, 5 and 6. We discuss the results of the experiments in Section 7 and conclude in Section 8.

2 Related work

Tumasjan et al. (2010) investigate how Twitter is used in political discourse and check if political sentiment on Twitter reflects real-life sentiments about parties and politicians. As a part of their study, they compare party mentions on Twitter with the results of the 2009 German parliament election. They conclude that the relative number of tweets mentioning a party is a good predictor for the number of votes of that party in an election. A similar finding was earlier reported by Jean Véronis in a series of blogposts: the number

[1]The data and software used for the experiments described in this paper can be retrieved from http://ifarm.nl/ps2011/p2011.zip

Proceedings of the 13th Conference of the European Chapter of the Association for Computational Linguistics, pages 53–60,
Avignon, France, April 23 - 27 2012. ©2012 Association for Computational Linguistics

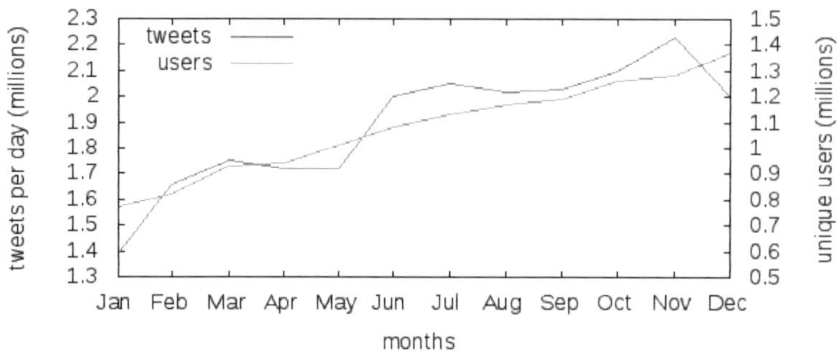

Figure 1: Overview of our collection of Dutch tweets of the year 2011. The data set contains almost 700 million tweets. Both the number of tweets (about two million per day) and the number of unique users (about one million) increase almost every month. The collection is estimated to contain about 37% of the total volume of Dutch tweets.

of times a French presidential candidate was mentioned in the press was a good prediction for his or her election results (Véronis, 2007). This prediction task involved only two candidates, so it was easier than predicting the outcome of a multiparty election.

Jungherr et al. (2011) criticize the work of Tumasjan et al. (2010). They argue that the choice of included parties in the evaluation was not well motivated and show that the inclusion of a seventh party, the Pirate Party, would have had a large negative effect on accuracy of the predictions. Furthermore, Jungherr et al. question the time period which was used by Tumasjan et al. for collecting the tweets and show that including the tweets of the week right before the election would also have had a significant negative effect on the prediction accuracy.

Using Twitter data for predicting election results was popular in 2010 and 2011. Chung and Mustafaraj (2011) found that merely counting tweets is not enough to obtain good predictions and measure the effect of sentiment analysis and spam filtering. O'Connor et al. (2010) discovered that while volumes of mentions of *obama* on Twitter before the US presidential election of 2008 correlated with high poll ratings for Barack Obama, volumes of mentions of his rival *mccain* also correlated with high poll ratings of the election winner. Gayo-Avello et al. (2011) show that predictions based on Twitter only predicted half of the winners of US congressional elections with two candidates correctly, a performance which is not better than chance.

3 Data collection

We collect Dutch Twitter messages (tweets) with the filter stream provided by Twitter. We continuously search for messages that contain at least one of a list of about a hundred high-frequent Dutch words and a dozen frequent Dutch subject tags (hashtags). The results of this process also contain some false positives: tweets that contain apparent Dutch words but are actually written in another language. In order to get rid of these messages, we apply a language guesser developed by Thomas Mangin (Mangin, 2007). It ranks languages by comparing character n-grams of an input text to n-gram models of texts in known languages. We use a set of 74 language models developed by our students in 2007.

In order to estimate the coverage of our selection with respect to all tweets in Dutch, we collected all tweets of one month from 1,017 randomly selected users which predominantly post messages in Dutch. We compared the two data streams and found that the first contained 37% of the data found in the second. This suggests that we collect about 37% of all Dutch tweets. Our data collection process contains two filters: one is based on a word list and the other is the language guesser. The first filter lost 62% of the data while the second lost another 1%.

Party	Short name	Long name	Total	Seats Twitter	Seats PB	Seats MdH	Average polls
PVV	2226	1	2227	18	12	12	12
VVD	1562	0	1562	13	14	16	15
CDA	1504	0	1504	12	9	10	9.5
PvdA	1056	1	1057	9	13	13	13
SP	839	0	839	7	8	7	7.5
GL	243	505	748	6	5	3	4
D66	610	0	610	5	6	5	5.5
CU	159	79	238	2	3	3	3
PvdD	103	51	154	1	1	1	1
SGP	139	0	139	1	2	2	2
50+	6	43	49	0	1	2	1.5
OSF	-	-	-	1	1	1	1
			offset	21	4	4	-

Table 1: Frequencies of tweets mentioning one of 11 main political parties from one day, Wednesday 16 February 2011, converted to Senate seats (column Seats Twitter) and compared with the predictions of two polls from the same week: from Politieke Barometer of 17 February (Synovate.nl, 2011b) and from Maurice de Hond of 15 February (Peil.nl, 2011b). The offset value is the sum of the differences between the Twitter predictions and the average poll predictions. The OSF group is a cooperation of 11 local parties which were not tracked on Twitter.

4 Counting party names

The Dutch Senate elections are held once every four years. The elections are preceded by the Dutch Provincial Election in which the voters choose 566 representatives for the States-Provincial. Three months later the new representatives elect the new Senate. In the second election, each of the representatives has a weight which is proportional to the number of people he or she represents. The 2011 Dutch provincial elections were held on Wednesday 2 March 2011 and the corresponding Senate elections were held on Monday 23 May 2011. In the Senate elections 75 seats are contested.

Our work on predicting the results of this election was inspired by the work of Tumasjan et al. (2010), who report that basic counts of tweets mentioning a political party provided good predictions for the results of the 2009 German parliament election. We decided to replicate their work for the Dutch Senate Elections of 2011.

We started with examining the Dutch tweets of Wednesday 16 February 2011, two weeks prior to the Provincial elections. This data set consisted of 1.7 million tweets. From this data set we extracted the tweets containing names of political parties. This resulted in 7,000 tweets. This number was lower than we had expected. Originally we had planned to use the tweets for predicting local election results. However, further filtering of the tweets to require location information would have left us with a total of about 70 political tweets per day, far too few to make reliable predictions for twelve different provinces.

In the data, we searched for two variants of each party: the abbreviated version and the full name, allowing for minor punctuation and capitalization variation. For nearly all parties, the abbreviated name was used more often on Twitter than the full name. The two exceptions are GroenLinks/GL and 50Plus/50+ (Table 1). Party names could be identified with a precision close to 100% except for the party ChristenUnie: its abbreviation CU is also used as slang for *see you*. This was the case for 11% of the tweets containing the phrase *CU*. In this paper, the 11% of tweets have already been removed from the counts of this party.

Apart from the eleven regular parties shown in Table 1, there was a twelfth party with a chance of winning a Senate seat: the Independent Senate Group (OSF), a cooperation of 11 regional parties. These parties occur infrequently in our Twitter data (less than five times per party per day), too infrequent to allow for a reliable base for predicting election results. Therefore we decided to use a baseline prediction for them. We assumed that the group would win exactly one Senate seat, just like in the two previous elections.

We converted the counts of the party names on Twitter to Senate seats by counting every tweet mentioning a party name as a vote for that party. The results can be found in the column *Seats Twitter* in Table 1. The predicted number of seats were compared with the results of two polls of the same week: one by the polling company Politieke Barometer of 17 February (Synovate.nl, 2011b) and another from the company Peil.nl, commonly referred to as Maurice de Hond, from 15 February (Peil.nl, 2011b). The predicted numbers of seats by Twitter were reasonably close to the numbers of the polling companies. However, there is room for improvement: for the party PVV, tweets predicted a total of 18 seats while the polling companies only predicted 12 and for the party 50+, Twitter predicted no seats while the average of the polling companies was 1.5 seats.

5 Normalizing party counts

The differences between the Twitter prediction and prediction of the polling companies could have been caused by noise. However, the differences could also have resulted from differences between the methods for computing the predictions. First, in the polls, like in an election, everyone has one vote. In the tweet data set this is not the case. One person may have send out multiple tweets or may have tweeted about different political parties. This problem of the data is easy to fix: we can keep only one political tweet per user in the data set and remove all others.

A second problem is that not every message containing a party name is necessarily positive about the party. For example:

> *Wel triest van de vvd om de zondagen nu te schrappen wat betreft het shoppen, jammer! Hierbij dus een #fail*
>
> *Sadly, the VVD will ban shopping on Sundays, too bad! So here is a #fail*

Party	One party per tweet	One tweet per user	Both constraints
PVV	22	17	19
VVD	12	13	13
CDA	12	12	12
PvdA	8	8	8
SP	6	8	7
GL	6	7	7
D66	5	5	5
CU	1	2	2
PvdD	1	1	1
SGP	1	1	0
50+	0	0	0
OSF	1	1	1
offset	29	22	25

Table 2: Senate seat predictions based on normalized tweets: keeping only tweets mentioning one party, keeping only the first tweet of each user and keeping of each user only the first tweet which mentioned a single party. The offset score is the seat difference between the predictions and the average poll prediction of Table 1.

While the tweet is mentioning a political party, the sender does not agree with the policy of the party and most likely will not vote for the party. These tweets need to be removed as well.

A third problem with the data is that the demographics of Dutch Twitter users are probably quite different from the demographics of Dutch voters. Inspection of Dutch tweets revealed that Twitter is very popular among Dutch teens but they are not eligible to vote. User studies for other countries have revealed that senior citizens are underrepresented on the Internet (Fox, 2010) but this group has a big turnout in elections (Epskamp and van Rhee, 2010). It would be nice if we could assign weights to tweets based on the representativeness of certain groups of users. Unfortunately we cannot determine the age and gender of individual Twitter users because users are not required to specify this information in their profile.

Based on the previous analysis, we tested two normalization steps for the tweet data. First, we removed all tweets that mentioned more than one party name. Next, we kept only the first tweet of each user. Finally we combined both steps: keeping of each user only the first tweet which mentioned a single political party. We converted all the counts to party seats and compared them with the poll outcomes. The results can be found in Table 2. The seat predictions did not improve. In fact, the offsets of the three methods proved to be larger than the corresponding number of the baseline approach without normalization (29, 25 and 22 compared to 21). Still, we believe that normalization of the tweet counts is a good idea.

Next, we determined the sentiments of the tweets. Since we do not have reliable automatic sentiment analysis software for Dutch, we decided to build a corpus of political tweets with manual sentiment annotation. Each of the two authors of this paper manually annotated 1,678 political tweets, assigning one of two classes to each tweet: negative towards the party mentioned in the tweet or nonnegative. The annotators agreed on the sentiment of 1,333 tweets (kappa score: 0.59).

We used these 1,333 tweets with unanimous class assignment for computing sentiment scores per party. We removed the tweets that mentioned more than one party and removed duplicate tweets of users that contributed more than one tweet. 534 nonnegative tweets and 227 negative tweets were left. Then we computed weights per party by dividing the number of nonnegative tweets per party by the associated total number of tweets. For example, there were 42 negative tweets for the VVD party and 89 nonnegative, resulting in a weight of 89/(42+89) = 0.68. The resulting party weights can be found in Table 3.

We multiplied the weights with the tweet counts obtained after the two normalization steps and converted these to Senate seats. As a result the difference with the poll prediction dropped from 25 to 23 (see Table 3). Incorporating sentiment analysis improved the results of the prediction.

After sentiment analysis, the tweets still did not predict the same number of seats as the polls for any party. For nine parties, the difference was two and a half seats or lower but the difference was larger for two parties: GL (5) and PvdA (6). A possible cause for these differences is a mismatch between the demographics of Twitter users

Party	Tweet count	Sentiment weight	Seats Twitter
PVV	811	0.49	13
VVD	552	0.68	13
CDA	521	0.70	12
PvdA	330	0.69	7
SP	314	0.90	9
GL	322	0.81	9
D66	207	0.94	6
CU	104	0.67	2
PvdD	63	1.00	2
SGP	39	0.86	1
50+	17	0.93	0
OSF	-	-	1
		offset	23

Table 3: Sentiment weights per party resulting from a manual sentiment analysis, indicating what fraction of tweets mentioning the party is nonnegative and the resulting normalized seat predictions after multiplying tweet counts with these weights. The second column contains the number of tweets per party after the normalization steps of Table 2.

and the Dutch population. We have no data describing this discrepancy. We wanted to build a model for this difference so we chose to model the difference by additional correction weights based on the seats differences between the two predictions. We based the expected number of seats on the two poll results of the same time period as the tweets (Synovate.nl, 2011b; Peil.nl, 2011b). For example, after normalization, there were 811 tweets mentioning the PVV party. The party has a sentiment weight of 0.49 so the adjusted number of tweets is 0.49*811 = 397. The polls predicted 12 of 74 seats for this party. The associated population weight is equal to the average number of poll seats divided by the total number of seats divided by the adjusted number of tweets divided by the total number of adjusted tweets (2,285): (12/74)/(397/2285) is 0.93.

The population weights can be found in Table 4. They corrected most predicted seat numbers of Twitter to the ones predicted by the polls. A drawback of this approach is that we have tuned the prediction system to the results of polls rather than to the results of elections. It would have been

Party	Population weight	Seats Twitter	Average polls
PVV	0.93	12	12
VVD	1.23	15	15
CDA	0.80	10	9.5
PvdA	1.76	13	13
SP	0.82	8	7.5
GL	0.47	4	4
D66	0.87	5	5.5
CU	1.33	3	3
PvdD	0.49	1	1
SGP	1.84	2	2
50+	2.93	1	1.5
OSF	-	1	1
	offset	2	-

Table 4: Population weights per party resulting from dividing the percentage of the predicted poll seats (Synovate.nl, 2011b; Peil.nl, 2011b) by the percentage of nonnegative tweets (Table 3), and the associated seat predictions from Twitter, which are now closer to the poll predictions. Offsets are measured by comparing with the average number of poll seats from Table 1.

Party	Result	Seats PB	Seats MdH	Seats Twitter
VVD	16	14	16	14
PvdA	14	12	11	16
CDA	11	9	9	8
PVV	10	11	12	10
SP	8	9	9	6
D66	5	7	5	8
GL	5	4	4	3
CU	2	3	3	3
50+	1	2	2	2
SGP	1	2	2	2
PvdD	1	1	2	2
OSF	1	1	0	1
offset	-	14	14	18

Table 5: Twitter seat prediction for the 2 March 2011 Dutch Senate elections compared with the actual results (Kiesraad.nl, 2012a) and the predictions of two polling companies of 1 March 2011: PB: Politieke Barometer (Synovate.nl, 2011a) and MdH: Maurice de Hond (Peil.nl, 2011a).

better to tune the system to the results of past elections but we do not have associated Twitter data for these elections. Adjusting the results of the system to get them as close to the poll predictions as possible, is the best we can do at this moment.

6 Predicting election outcomes

The techniques described above were applied to Dutch political tweets collected in the week before the election: 23 February 2011 – 1 March 2011: 64,395 tweets. We used a week of data rather than a day because we expected that using more data would lead to better predictions. We chose for a week of tweets rather than a month because we assumed that elections were not an important discussion topic on Twitter one month before they were held.

After the first two normalization steps, one party per tweet and one tweet per user, 28,704 tweets were left. The parties were extracted from the tweets, and counted, and the counts were multiplied with the sentiment and population weights and converted to Senate seats. The results are shown in Table 5 together with poll predictions (Synovate.nl, 2011a; Peil.nl, 2011a) and the results of the elections of 2 March 2011 (Kiesraad.nl, 2012a).

The seat numbers predicted by the tweets were close to the election results. Twitter predicted the correct number of seats for the party PVV while the polling companies predicted an incorrect number. However the companies predicted other seat numbers correctly and they had a smaller total error: 14 seats compared to 18 for our approach.

In Dutch elections, there is no strict linear relation between the number of votes for a party and the number seats awarded to a party. Seats that remain after truncating seat numbers are awarded to parties by a system which favors larger parties (Kiesraad.nl, 2012b). Furthermore, in 2011 there was a voting incident in the Senate elections which caused one party (D66) to loose one of its seats to another party (SP). In our evaluation we have compared seat numbers because that is the only type of data that we have available from the polling companies. The election results allow a comparison based on percentages of votes. This comparison is displayed in Table 6.

Party	Result	Twitter	offset
VVD	19.6%	17.3%	-2.3%
PvdA	17.3%	20.8%	+3.5%
CDA	14.1%	11.0%	-3.1%
PVV	12.4%	13.3%	+0.9%
SP	10.2%	8.5%	-1.7%
D66	8.4%	10.1%	+1.7%
GL	6.3%	4.8%	-1.5%
CU	3.6%	4.0%	+0.4%
50+	2.4%	3.1%	+0.7%
SGP	2.4%	3.1%	+0.7%
PvdD	1.9%	2.7%	+0.8%
OSF	1.4%	1.3%	-0.1%
offset	-	17.4%	

Table 6: Twitter vote prediction for the 2 March 2011 Dutch Provincial elections compared with the actual results in percentages[2].

Party	Result	Seats Twitter	Population weight
VVD	16	16	2.23
PvdA	14	13	1.93
CDA	11	10	1.41
PVV	10	12	1.78
SP	8	7	1.11
D66	5	5	0.82
GL	5	4	0.59
CU	2	3	0.45
50+	1	1	0.22
SGP	1	2	0.30
PvdD	1	1	0.15
OSF	1	1	-
offset	-	8	

Table 7: Seat prediction for the 2 March 2011 Dutch Senate elections based on an uniform distribution of tweets mentioning political parties.

With the exception of the three largest parties, all predicted percentages are within 1.7% of the numbers of the election. The percentages might prove to be more reliable than seat numbers as a base for a election prediction method. We hope to use percentage figures when the predicting the outcome of next parliament elections: one of the polling companies publishes such figures with their predictions of parliament elections.

7 Discussion

Although we are happy about the accuracy obtained by the Twitter predictions, we have some concerns about the chosen approach. In Table 4, we introduced poll-dependent weights to correct the demographic differences between the Twitter users and the Dutch electorate. This was necessary because we did not have information about the demographics of Twitter users, for example about their gender and age. As already mentioned, this choice led to tuning the system to predicting poll results rather than election results. But do the population weights not also minimize the effect that tweet counts have on the predictions? Does the system still use the tweet counts for the election prediction?

In order to answer the latter question, we designed an additional experiment. Suppose the tweets per party were uniformly distributed such that each party name appeared in the same number of tweets each day. This would make tweet counts uninteresting for predicting elections. However, how would our system deal with this situation? The results of this experiment are shown in Table 7.

Since we did not have data to base sentiment weights on, we assumed that all the sentiment weights had value 1.0. Since the tweet counts were different from those in the earlier experiments, we needed to compute new population weights (see Table 7). The seat numbers predicted by the system were equal to the average of the seat numbers of the two polls in Table 4 plus or minus a half in case the two numbers added up to an odd number. The VVD party gained one seat, as a consequence of the system of awarding remainder seats to larger parties. We assume that the tweet distribution will be uniform at all times and this means that the system will always predict the seat distribution. The offset of the new prediction was 3 seats for the test distribution of Table 4 and 8 seats for the election results (see Table 7), a

[2]CU and SGP were awarded an additional 0.3% and 0.2% for the 0.5% they won as an alliance.

smaller error than either of the polling companies (compare with Table 5).

This experiment has produced a system which generates the average of the predictions of the two polling companies from the week of 16/17 February as an election prediction. It does not require additional input. This is not a good method for predicting election outcome but by chance it generated a better prediction than our earlier approach and those of two polling companies. We are not sure what conclusions to draw from this. Is the method of using population weights flawed? Is our evaluation method incorrect? Are tweets bad predictors of political sentiment? Is the margin of chance error large? It would be good to test whether the measured differences are statistically significant but we do not know how to do that for this data.

8 Concluding remarks

We have collected a large number of Dutch Twitter messages (hundreds of millions) and showed how they can be used for predicting the results of the Dutch Senate elections of 2011. Counting the tweets that mention political parties is not sufficient to obtain good predictions. We tested the effects of improving the quality of the data collection by removing certain tweets: tweets mentioning more than one party name, multiple tweets from a single user and tweets with a negative sentiment. Despite having no gold standard training data, the total error of our final system was only 29% higher than that of two experienced polling companies (Table 5). We hope to improve these results in the future, building on the knowledge we have obtained in this study.

Acknowledgements

We would like to thank the two reviewers of this paper for valuable comments.

References

Jessica Chung and Eni Mustafaraj. 2011. Cam collective sentiment expressed on twitter predict political elections? In *Proceedings of the Twenty-Fifth AAAI Conference on Artificial Intelligence*. San Francisco, CA, USA.

Martijn Epskamp and Marn van Rhee. 2010. Analyse opkomst gemeenteraadsverkiezingen 2010.

Susannah Fox. 2010. Four in ten seniors go online. Pew Research Center, http://www.pewinternet.org /Commentary/2010/January/38-of-adults-age-65-go-online.aspx (Retrieved 8 March 2012).

Daniel Gayo-Avello, Panagiotis Metaxas, and Eni Mustafaraj. 2011. Limits of electoral predictions using social media data. In *Proceedings of the International AAAI Conference on Weblogs and Social Media*. Barcelona, Spain.

Andreas Jugherr, Pascal Jürgens, and Harald Schoen. 2011. Why the pirate party won the german election of 2009 or the trouble with predictions: A response to tumasjan, a., sprenger, t. o., sander, p. g., & welpe, i. m. 'predicting elections with twitter: What 140 characters reveal about political sentiment'. *Social Science Computer Review*.

Kiesraad.nl. 2012a. Databank verkiezingsuitslagen. http://www.verkiezingsuitslagen.nl/Na1918/Verkiezingsuitslagen.aspx?VerkiezingsTypeId=2 (retrieved 27 February 2012).

Kiesraad.nl. 2012b. Toewijzing zetels. http://www.kiesraad.nl/nl/Onderwerpen/Uitslagen/Toewijzing_zetels.html (retrieved 27 February 2012).

Thomas Mangin. 2007. ngram: Textcat implementation in python. http://thomas.mangin.me.uk/.

Brendan O'Connor, Ramnath Balasubramanyan, Bryan R. Routledge, and Noah A. Smith. 2010. From tweets to polls: Linking text sentiment to public opinion time series. In *Proceedings of the International AAAI Conference on Weblogs and Social Media*. Washington DC, USA.

Peil.nl. 2011a. Nieuw haags peil 1 maart 2011. http://www.peil.nl/?3182 (retrieved 5 March 2012).

Peil.nl. 2011b. Nieuw haags peil 15 februari 2011. http://www.peil.nl/?3167 (retrieved 1 March 2012).

Synovate.nl. 2011a. Nieuws 2011 - peiling eerste kamer - week 9. http://www.synovate.nl/content.asp? targetid=721 (retrieved 5 March 2012).

Synovate.nl. 2011b. Peiling eerste kamer - week 7. http://www.synovate.nl/content.asp?targetid=713 (retrieved 5 March 2012).

Andranik Tumasjan, Timm Sprenger, Philipp Sandner, and Isabell Welpe. 2010. Predicting elections with twitter: What 140 characters reveal about political sentiment. In *Proceedings of the Fourth AAAI conference on Weblogs and Social Media*, pages 178–185.

Jean Véronis. 2007. 2007: La presse fait á nouveau mieux que les sondeurs. http://blog.veronis.fr /2007/05/2007-la-presse-fait-nouveau-mieux-que.html.

Opinion and Suggestion Analysis for Expert Recommendations

Anna Stavrianou and **Caroline Brun**
Xerox Research Centre Europe
6, chemin de Maupertuis
38240 Meylan, France
{anna.stavrianou,caroline.brun}@xrce.xerox.com

Abstract

In this paper, we propose the use of fine-grained information such as opinions and suggestions extracted from users' reviews about products, in order to improve a recommendation system. While typical recommender systems compare a user profile with some reference characteristics to rate unseen items, they rarely make use of the content of reviews users have done on a given product. In this paper, we show how we applied an opinion extraction system to extract opinions but also suggestions from the content of the reviews, use the results to compare other products with the reviewed one, and eventually recommend a better product to the user.

1 Introduction

Social media has enabled web users to interact through social platforms, express their opinions, comment and review various products/items. Such user-generated content has been analysed from a social as well as content-oriented point of view. For instance, social network analysis techniques have been used to identify user roles (Agarwal et al., 2008; Domingos and Richardson, 2001; Fisher et al., 2006; Zhang et al., 2007) and text or opinion mining techniques have been applied to identify positive/negative tendencies within user online review comments (Ding and Liu, 2007; Ghose et al., 2007; Hu and Liu, 2004; Leskovec et al., 2010). In the applicative context, recommender systems (Adomavicius and Tuzhilin, 2005) make use of the opinion information (such as in star-rating systems) and recommend items (movies, products, news articles, etc.) or social elements (i.e. propositions to connect with other people or communities), that are likely to be of interest to a specific user.

Typically, a recommender system compares a user profile with some reference characteristics, and seeks to predict the "preference" or "rating" that a user would give to an item not yet considered. These characteristics may be part of the information item (the content-based approach) or the user's social environment (the collaborative filtering approach). Comments published on social networking or review web sites are sometimes used by recommender systems (Aciar et al., 2007; Jakob et al., 2009) in order to find out similarities between users that comment on the same items in the same way. However, extracting explicit semantic information carried out in these comments (e.g. "this printer is slow") is of great interest in order to detect what a user has liked or disliked about a given topic (e.g. the speed of the printer) and consequently take it into account to make recommendations.

In this paper, we propose the extraction of opinions and suggestions from user reviews or free text and their use as input information to improve recommender systems. This technique could be used on top of standard recommender techniques in order to further fine-grain the recommendation according to the user comments.

To the best of our knowledge, no existing approach takes advantage of the fine-grained opinions or suggestions the user **explicitly** expresses using natural language within a review or a free text. As aforementioned, some works consider the product reviews as a means to get user opinions on certain products and use this information for recommendation purposes. Nevertheless, they all assign a polarity ("negative" or "positive") to

Proceedings of the 13th Conference of the European Chapter of the Association for Computational Linguistics, pages 61–69,
Avignon, France, April 23 - 27 2012. ©2012 Association for Computational Linguistics

the review or they update the rating (e.g. giving a value from 1 to 5) without going further down exploiting the exact phrases. More particularly they do not detect what aspects of the product have been appreciated or not. For example, no approach considers using the user-stated phrase "I would prefer a lighter camera" in order to recommend to a user a camera that satisfies all the desired features and on top of this being lighter than the reviewed one.

The paper continues with a state-of-the art discussion. Section 3 is divided into two parts; a description of the methodology followed in order to extract opinion information from reviews through NLP techniques and a description of how this information is used for recommending product items. Section 4 shows an example and Section 5 presents a first attempt of an evaluation. Section 6 concludes and discusses future work.

2 Related Work

Although there are no works that use the explicit semantics extracted from reviews for recommendation purposes, our approach has some similarities with the analysis of reviews state-of-the-art.

Identifying the opinion of customer reviews has concerned different research communities. Some significant works infer opinion polarities based on comparisons with a pre-defined seed-list of adjectives (Ding and Liu, 2007; Hu and Liu, 2004) or implicitly through observing the changes in the respective product prices of reputation systems (Ghose et al., 2007). An attempt of extracting suggestions (and not just opinions) from customer reviews has also been presented in (Vishwanath and Aishwarya, 2011), in which ontologies and feedback rules are used for this purpose.

Combining knowledge of opinions extracted from reviews and recommender systems has also some applications. For example, (Jakob et al., 2009), have analysed opinions of movie reviews. They use pre-defined categories of movie features (acting, production, soundtrack, cinematography and storyline), and they assign polarities (negative or positive) to each category according to the per-feature opinion words expressed for each review. For example, if a movie review contains the sentence "the acting is flat", they assign a negative polarity to the category "acting" and they just avoid recommending the specific movie to the users. They do not explicitly use the opinion information in order to make comparisons with similar movies and propose one "less flat" to the user.

Similarly to (Jakob et al., 2009), most research works that use opinion information for recommendation purposes consider only the polarity and not the explicit semantics of the opinions. For instance, in (Aciar et al., 2007) or (Poirier, 2011) they assign a kind of "rating" on each review regarding the product. Comparisons are not included.

(Sun et al., 2009) include opinion-based and feature-based comparisons in order to recommend products to users. Their approach takes into account a whole set of reviews (as opposed to individual ones) and it involves no NLP parsing. The opinions are aggregated into a sentiment value and this value points out mainly whether a product feature is better or not when it comes to comparing different models of the same product.

NLP techniques have, in some cases, been used for recommendation. As an example, in the paper of (Chai et al., 2002) the user can "chat" with the system in order to describe what type of product she desires, receiving in return a list of recommended products. Although, in this case, comparisons between products take place in the database, opinion identification is not included. The user neither expresses a complaint nor she suggests an improvement, thus, no opinion detection takes place.

3 Opinion mining for expert recommendations

In this section we describe the approach followed in order to initially parse the user reviews regarding manufactured products, extract opinion information from them and, then, use this information for the purpose of providing expert recommendations.

Each product review concerns one specific product whose brand and model are clearly mentioned each time. In web sites such as "epinions.com" this information appears in the title of the review and it is straightforward to extract. In order to make use of the content of the reviews, we apply a system relying on a deep semantic analysis that detects opinions and suggestions within the customer reviews. Natural language techniques allow the detection of the weaknesses of the product (focusing on specific features) or the potential improvements, according to the user's point of view.

The information extracted from the reviews is then confronted to a database of products containing information such as product characteristics, usage details, average price, etc. For the purposes of this paper, we consider only product characteristics whose values can be boolean or numeric and as such they can be compared with the traditional methods. The system selects, within this database, one or more similar products that compensate for the problems or improvement needs identified within the review. Then, pointers to these products can be explicitly associated with the specific review as "expert recommendations", and constitute an automatic enrichment of the review.

The advantage for readers of these enriched reviews is to benefit from a contextualized recommendation that takes into account the semantic information conveyed in reviews of people who have used a given product. Moreover, the review's reader may be helped in her product search and may have a recommendation on a product she did not even know it exists. Figure 1 shows a schema of the process followed which is explained in more detail in the next sections.

3.1 Semantic Extraction

Our approach begins with the extraction of semantic information from each review and more specifically the identification of the user's suggestion(s) and/or opinion(s) together with the product features and respective comparison words.

For the purpose of identifying the weaknesses or the possible improvements mentioned in the text, we need to extract the opinion of a user about a given characteristic of a product. Thus, we apply an opinion detection system that is able to perform feature-based opinion mining, relating the main concept (e.g. a printer) to several features (e.g. quality, print speed and resolution), that can be evaluated separately.

Formally, our system adopts the representation of a given opinion as proposed by (Liu, 2010), where an opinion is a five place predicate of the form $(o_j, f_jk, s_ijkl, h_i, t_l)$, where:

- o_j is the target object of the opinion (the main concept)
- f_jk is a feature associated to the object
- s_ijkl is the value (positive or negative) of the opinion expressed by the opinion holder about the feature
- h_i is the opinion holder
- t_l is the time when the opinion is expressed.

The opinion extraction system is designed on top of the XIP robust syntactic parser (Aït-Mokhtar et al., 2002), which is used as a fundamental component, in order to extract deep syntactic dependencies, from which semantic relations of opinion are calculated. These semantic relations are intermediary steps to instantiate the five place predicates which are compliant with the aforementioned model. Having syntactic relations already extracted by a general dependency grammar, we use the robust parser by combining lexical information about word polarities, subcategorization information and syntactic dependencies to extract the semantic relations that will then instantiate this model.

There exist other systems, such as the one described in (Kim and Hovy, 2006), that use syntactic dependencies to link the source and target of the opinions. Our system (Brun, 2011) belongs to this family, since we believe that the syntactic processing of complex phenomena (negation, comparison and anaphora) is a necessary step in order to perform feature-based opinion mining. Another characteristic of our system is that it respects a two-level architecture; it relies on a generic level, applicable to all domains and corpora, and on a domain-dependent level, adapted for each sub-domain of application.

Moreover, our system includes a semantic mapping between polar vocabulary and the features it corresponds to. For instance, the opinion word "fast" is mapped to the feature "speed", the word "expensive" to the feature "price", the word "clunk" to "noise" and so on. This mapping enables us to further exploit the comments of the user by referring to specific product characteristics.

When analyzing an example like *"The photo quality of my prints is astonishing. This printer is really not that expensive."*, our system extracts two relations of opinion :

- OPINION_POSITIVE(astonishing,photo quality): the dependency parser extracts an

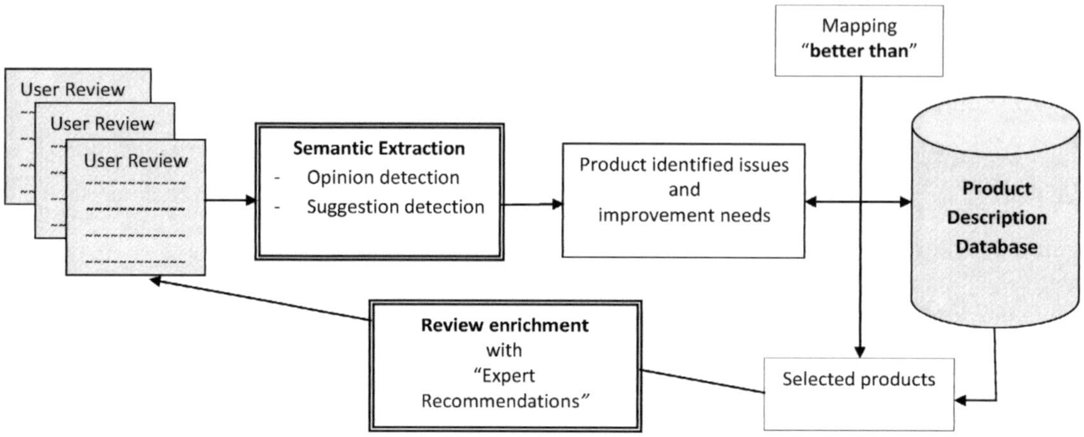

Figure 1: Extracting opinion semantic information from product reviews and provide expert recommendations.

attributive syntactic relation between the subject *"photo quality"* and the positive adjectival attribute *"astonishing"* from which this relation of opinion is inferred about the feature *"photo quality"*

- OPINION_POSITIVE(expensive,printer): the dependency parser also extracts an attributive syntactic relation between the subject *"printer"* and the negative adjective attribute *"expensive"*, but it also extracts a negation on the main verb: the polarity of the final relation is inverted, i.e. is finally positive. As we have also encoded that the adjective *"expensive"* is semantically linked to *"price"*, this opinion is linked to the feature *"price"*.

In addition, the system includes a specific detection of suggestions of improvements, which goes beyond the scope of traditional opinion detection. Suggestions of improvements are expressed with two discursive figures denoting "wishes" or "regrets". To detect these specific discurse patterns, we use again information extracted by the parser, i.e. syntactic relations such as SUBJECT, OBJECT, MODIFIER, but also information about verbal tenses, modality and verbal aspect, combined with terminological information about the domain, in our case, the domain of printers.

Some examples follow that show what the system would output considering certain input sentences extracted from customer reviews about printers:

1. *Input*: "I think they should have put a faster scanner on the machine, one at least as fast as the printer."
   Output:
   SUGGESTION_IMPROVE(scanner, speed)

   In this example, the system identifies from the input sentence that the user is not satisfied with the speed of the scanner and would have liked it to be quicker.

2. *Input*: "I like this printer, but I think it is too expensive."
   Output: OPINION_POSITIVE(printer, _), OPINION_NEGATIVE(printer, price).

   In this example, the system identifies that the user is not happy with the price of the printer although the rest of its characteristics satisfy him.

3. *Input*: "The problem of this printer is the fuser."
   Output:
   OPINION_NEGATIVE(printer, fuser).

   In this example, the system identifies that the problem lies in the fuser of the printer.

The first two examples can be further exploited by the approach we propose. For instance, for the second example, the reader of this review could benefit from a recommendation of a similar but cheaper printer. The third example contains information that is not measured (it has neither boolean nor numeric values) and as such it is out of the scope of this paper.

3.2 Review enrichment

Following the detection of the opinions or suggestions regarding specific product features, we identify products that match the non-mentioned or positive characteristics of the reviewed product while at the same time satisfying the user suggestions.

We consider a database that stores products together with their features. Same type of products are stored similarly for evident reasons. The database can be populated either manually or automatically through the web sites that hold product information and it needs to be updated so that new products appear and old ones are never recommended. Access to the database is done through standard SQL queries.

The system retrieves products of the same usage (e.g. a user that is reading a review for a PC laptop will not need a recommendation for a PC desktop), while selecting those ones whose features are within the same or "better" range. The features that should definitely be in "better" range are the ones retrieved with the help of the opinion detection system described previously. These features would be suggestions or negative opinions the user has expressed about a product.

The ranges can be defined in many ways and they can be subject to change. For example, the prices may be considered to change ranges every 50 Euro or 500 Euro depending on the average price of the product. The feature requested by the user (e.g. "cheaper") should have a value in a different range in order to really satisfy her this time (e.g. a computer that costs 5 Euro less than the reviewed one is not really considered as "cheaper").

Defining what "better" range refers to, depends on the feature. For instance, the lower the price, the better it is, whereas, the higher the speed the better. In order to avoid this confusion we keep the descending (e.g. in the case of price) or ascending (e.g. in the case of speed) semantics of the feature within the database.

Once the system has identified the products that seem to be closer to the user requirements, it highlights these products by presenting them as "expert recommendations". These recommendations may appear on each review as enrichments assuming that the characteristics not mentioned as negative by the user have satisfied her, so she would be happy with a similar product having basically the mentioned features improved. The recommendation is mainly useful to the reader of the review that is in the decision process before buying a product.

Some special - sometimes often appearing - matching cases worth mentioning:

Multiple features: If more than one feature needs to be improved, priorities can be defined dependent on the order in which the features are mentioned in the review.

No comparable features: for this paper features are taken into account only if they are numeric or boolean (presence/absence) and can be subjectively compared.

Many matching products: more than one product can be recommended. The limit of the number of products can be pre-defined and the products may appear to the user in the order of less-to-more expensive.

No better answer: if no product is found that may satisfy the user then the search can go on in products of a different brand. The system has also the choice to remain "silent" and give no recommendation.

A non-demanded feature changes: in the case that a requested product is found but it is more expensive than the reviewed product, the recommendation would include some information regarding this feature (e.g. "A proposed product is "..." whose price, though, is higher").

4 Example

Before evaluating our approach we present an example that shows the semantic extraction and recommendation process. We consider a small set of printers together with their characteristics and prices. These data are taken from epinions.com at a date just before the submission of this paper. The data appear in Table 1 in descending order of price.

Brand	Model	Usage	Technology	Black speed	Capacity	Price($)
X	8560 Laser	Workgroup	Color	30	1675	930
X	6360V Laser	Workgroup	Color	42	1250	754
X	6180 Laser	Workgroup	Color	26	300	750
X	4118 All-in-One Laser	All-in-One	Monochrome	18	650	747
HP	Laserjet Cp2025n	Workgroup	Color	20	300	349
HP	Laserjet M1212nf	All-in-One	Monochrome	19	150	139

Table 1: Printer information used for the purposes of the example(source: www.epinions.com).

In the examples that follow, the input is a sentence that is assumed to be in the review of a given product.

1. Review about the "6180 Laser" printer. *Input*:"I think they should have allowed for a higher capacity."

   Semantic Extraction step:
   SUGGESTION_IMPROVE(printer, capacity)

   Identify similar products step:

   - identify reviewed characteristics: workgroup, laser, color, 26 ppm black speed, 300 sheets capacity, $750 price
   - identify similar printers where capacity is higher (next range) than 300 sheets

   Expert recommendation: A proposed printer with a higher capacity is the "6360V Laser Printer".

2. Review about the "6180 Laser" printer. *Input*:"I like it but it is expensive!"

   Semantic Extraction step:
   OPINION_NEGATIVE(printer, price)

   Identify similar products step:

   - identify reviewed characteristics: workgroup, laser, color, 26 ppm black speed, 300 sheets capacity, $750 price
   - identify similar printers where price is lower than $750.

   Expert recommendation: A proposed cheaper printer of the same type is "HP, LaserJet Cp2025n".

5 Evaluation

The evaluation of the proposed system concerns two modules; the semantic extraction and the review enrichment.

The first module has already been evaluated previously showing encouraging results. The system has been evaluated as to whether it correctly classifies the reviews according to the overall opinion. The structure of the "epinions.com" web site has been used for the evaluation since each author has tagged the respective review with a tag "recommended" or "not recommended", the corpus can be thus considered as annotated for classification. The SVM classifier (Joachims, 1998) has been used with a training set of opinions extracted by our system from 313 reviews and a test set of 2735 reviews, giving a 93% accuracy.

The review enrichment module evaluation, presented in this paper, focuses on whether the recommended products enrich the specific review and may satisfy the user by improving at least one of the negative features mentioned or following a specified suggestion without worsen the range of the rest of the features. The experiments are run against a database of 5,772 printers whose details are extracted from the "epinions.com" site.

For the purposes of this evaluation, we have developed a product comparison module that takes as input, for our case, the reviewed printer model together with the opinion and suggestion relations as extracted by the opinion mining system. The output of the comparison module is a set of recommended printers which are similar to the reviewed one while improving the negative features (based on a comparison of the feature values).

The comparison module deals with features that are numeric or boolean (presence/absence). Printers are queried against their type (color-laser/inkjet, personal/workgroup, etc.), their functions (copier, scanner etc.) and their features (speed, resolution, etc.). Ranges have been defined according to the average per-feature-ranges that are in the database. These ranges can be extended according to the number of recommendations we would like to have (the larger the range the more the recommendations).

Certain assumptions have been made in order to provide the recommendations. One such assumption is that the author of the review knows how to best make use of the printer she has bought. For example, if the user is complaining about the printer's resolution or print quality, we assume that she makes her printing decisions (paper size, landscape/portrait) based on her knowledge of the printer's resolution. Thus, the specific review can indeed be enriched with a recommendation of a printer with a better resolution rather than an advice on how to use the specific printer (e.g. by using a different media size).

Furthermore, certain issues had to be taken care of such as missing data and different measurement units that are not necessarily comparable. When the values of the features that are to be improved are missing, the respective products are not taken into account. The missing data case is also applied when the same feature is measured in different units between two similar products. At a later stage we may include such products in the recommendations and inform the user about the differences.

The experiments were run over 129 printer reviews from the "epinions.com" site containing negative opinions and/or suggestions. The reviews concerned 6 different brands while the database from which the recommended products are extracted contains printers from 14 different brands. Once the need-to-be improved features were extracted from the reviews, the comparison module was run in order to identify the recommended products.

The recommendation output is manually evaluated by looking at the technical features on the one side and by looking at the reviews of the recommended model on the other. It has to be noted that this is a first evaluation of the system having the usual problems that recommender systems evaluations have e.g. recall calculations, finding the right experts etc. Since we have used a printer dataset, the ideal experts to validate whether we propose better or not printers would be experts from the field of printers. Not having found such experts at the moment, we limit our evaluations to the following two-faceted one:

Feature-based evaluation: Based on the feature values, our system has a 100% precision, meaning that the recommended products are indeed similar to the reviewed ones while improving at least one of the required features. As a result, in all cases the recommended products are technically better than the reviewed one and they can help in the review enrichment.

Rating-based evaluation: In order to see whether an average user could benefit from such a recommendation, we have also evaluated our approach by looking at the reviews of the recommended products. This evaluation is quite limited, though, because not all recommended products have had reviews.
Thus, we took into account only the recommended products that have had a review. We used the average rating values of the "epinions.com" site which is a rating that considers the number of reviews together with the star-system ratings. These average ratings range from "disappointing", "ok", "very good" and "excellent". For each product we accept the recommended products that have a rating other than "disappointing" which is at least as good as the product's rating.
Only 32 products out of the 129 reviewed were used because those were the ones which had an average rating value on the web site. The accuracy we have achieved is 80.34%. In Figure 2 the percentage of accepted versus rejected recommendations is shown per brand. The brand names are replaced by numbers.

Finally, we would like to point out that in printer reviews people complain mostly about issues that do not involve comparable features (e.g. paper jams, toner problems) or that are not given as part of the detailed characteristics (e.g. cartridge prices). As such, in the future, we would like to use a different product dataset/review-set to run the experiment over.

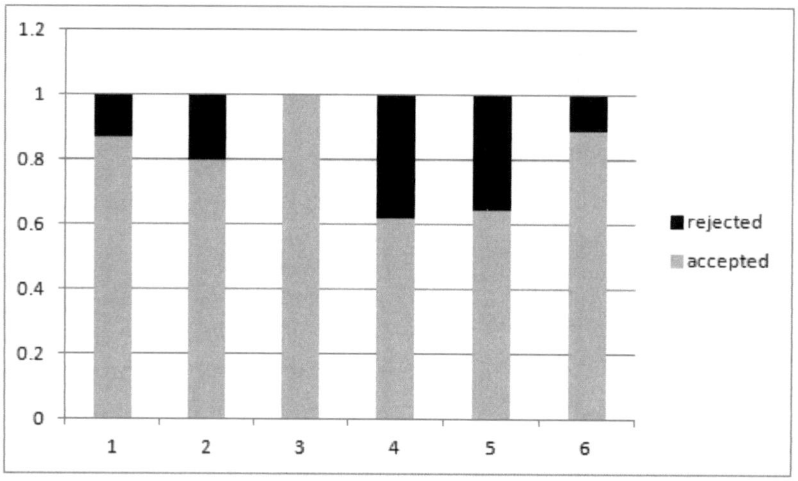

Figure 2: Rating-based evaluation results: rejected versus accepted recommendations over a number of different brands.

6 Conclusion

In this paper, we propose using written opinions and suggestions that are automatically extracted from user web reviews as input to a recommender system. This kind of opinions is analysed from a syntactic and semantic point of view and is used as a means to recommend items "better than" the reviewed one.

The novelty of our proposal lies in the fact that the semantics of opinions hidden in social media such as user reviews have not been explicitly used in order to generate recommendations. To the best of our knowledge, using the explicit comments of a user in order to enrich the reviews in a contextual manner has not yet appeared in literature.

In the future, our system could also consider the user's role knowledge (e.g. expert or novice) in order to consider her suggestion from a different weighted-point-of-view. An expert may have already looked at certain existing products before buying something so she may need a more original or diverse recommendation provided. The role of the user could potentially be identified through the social network he is in (if there is one).

We realise that some reviews may be spam or they may be written by non-trustworthy users. However, our approach aims at providing expert recommendations as a response to a single review by considering only what is mentioned in this specific review. This means that the content of a review, even if it is spam, will not be used in order to provide recommendations for another review.

References

Silvana Aciar, Debbie Zhang, Simeon Simoff, and John Debenham. 2007. Informed recommender: Basing recommendations on consumer product reviews. *IEEE Intelligent Systems*, 22(3).

Gediminas Adomavicius and Alexander Tuzhilin. 2005. Towards the next generation of recommender systems: a survey of the state-of-the-art and possible extensions. *IEEE Transactions on Knowledge and Data Engineering*, 17(6):734–749.

Nitin Agarwal, Huan Liu, Lei Tang, and Philip S. Yu. 2008. Identifying the influential bloggers in a community. In *WSDM '08: Proceedings of the international conference on Web search and web data mining*, pages 207–218, New York, NY, USA. ACM.

Salah Aït-Mokhtar, Jean-Pierre Chanod, and Claude Roux. 2002. Robustness beyond shallowness: incremental deep parsing. *Nat. Lang. Eng.*, 8:121–144, June.

Caroline Brun. 2011. Detecting opinions using deep syntactic analysis. In *Recent Advances in Natural Language Processing (RANLP)*.

Joyce Chai, Veronika Horvath, Nicolas Nicolov, Stys Margo, Nanda Kambhatla, Wlodek Zadrozny, and Prem Melville. 2002. Natural language assistant: A dialog system for online product recommendation. *AI Magazine*, 23(2).

Xiaowen Ding and Bing Liu. 2007. The utility of linguistic rules in opinion mining. In *SIGIR-07*.

Pedro Domingos and Matt Richardson. 2001. Mining the network value of customers. In *SIGKDD*, pages 57–66.

Danyel Fisher, Marc Smith, and Howard T. Welser. 2006. You are who you talk to: Detecting roles in usenet newsgroups. In *Proceedings of the 39th Annual Hawaii International Conference on System Sciences*, pages 59b–59b.

Anindya Ghose, Panagiotis G. Ipeirotis, and Arun Sundararajan. 2007. Opinion mining using econometrics: a case study on reputation systems. In *ACL*.

Minqing Hu and Bing Liu. 2004. Mining and summarizing customer reviews. In *KDD 04*, pages 168–177. ACM.

Niklas Jakob, Stefan Hagen Weber, Mark Christoph Müller, and Iryna Gurevych. 2009. Beyond the stars: Exploiting free-text user reviews to improve the accuracy of movie recommendations. In *CIKM Workshop on Topic-Sentiment Analysis for Mass Opinion*.

Thorsten Joachims. 1998. Text categorization with support vector machines: learning with many relevant features. In *10th European Conference on Machine Learning (ECML)*, page 137142.

Soo-Min Kim and Eduard Hovy. 2006. Identifying and analyzing judgment opinions. In *Proceedings of the main conference on Human Language Technology Conference of the North American Chapter of the Association of Computational Linguistics*, HLT-NAACL '06, pages 200–207, Stroudsburg, PA, USA. Association for Computational Linguistics.

Jure Leskovec, Daniel P. Huttenlocher, and Jon M. Kleinberg. 2010. Predicting positive and negative links in online social networks. In *WWW*, pages 641–650.

Bing Liu. 2010. Sentiment analysis and subjectivity. *Handbook of Natural Language Processing*, 2nd ed.

Damien Poirier. 2011. From text to recommendation (des textes communautaires a la recommandation). *PhD Dissertation*.

Jianshu Sun, Chong Long, Xiaoyan Zhu, and Minlie Huang. 2009. Mining reviews for product comparison and recommendation. *Polibits*, 39:33–40.

J. Vishwanath and S. Aishwarya. 2011. User suggestions extraction from customer reviews. *International Journal on Computer Science and Engineering*, 3(3).

Jun Zhang, Mark S. Ackerman, and Lada Adamic. 2007. Expertise networks in online communities: Structure and algorithms. In *Proceedings of the 16th International conference on World Wide Web*, pages 221–230.

Author Index

Barbosa, Denilson, 28
Bos, Johan, 53
Brun, Caroline, 61

Celli, Fabio, 10
Codina-Filba, Joan, 46

Darling, William M., 1

El-Hachem, Jinan, 37

Gao, Dehong, 18
Grivolla, Jens, 46

Haarslev, Volker, 37
Husby, Stephanie, 28

Li, Wenjie, 18

Paul, Michael J., 1

Rodriguez-Penagos, Carlos, 46
Rossi, Luca, 10

Song, Fei, 1
Stavrianou, Anna, 61

Tjong Kim Sang, Erik, 53

Zhang, Renxian, 18

Association for Computational Linguistics
209 N. Eighth Street
Stroudsburg, Pennsylvania 18360

CURRAN ASSOCIATES INC
proceedings.com